Intention, Practice and Achievement in the Poetic Drama of W.B. Yeats and T.S. Eliot

By
Minakshi Poddar

CLASSIC PUBLICATIONS
JAIPUR

Intention, Practice and Achievement in the Poetic Drama of W.B. Yeats and T.S. Eliot

Dr. Minakshi Poddar

First Published - 1998

ISBN : 81-87068-13-2

Published by :

CLASSIC PUBLICATIONS
260-61, Chaura Rasta, Jaipur-302 003 India

Printed in India at :

Vaishali Off-Set Pvt. Ltd.
Vaishali Nagar, Jaipur

Foreword

Much of good Research work in our country remains unknown as it is not published. Currently the Publishers don't take interest in this venture it does not seem profitable. As a result the academic world is deprived of the benefit that should accrue of the research.

The Vidyapeth has decided that publication of all good research work at the Institute will be its responsibility.

The provision of unassigned grant by the University Grants Commission has helped the Vidyapith considerably in making this resolve of its possible. Classic Publications, Jaipur has extended its help in wide distribution of the published work. The Vidyapith is grateful to the Commission and the Publisher for their help.

Banasthali

Diwakar Shastri
Secretary
Banasthali Vidyapith

Acknowledgments

It is not possible for me to express adequately my sense of gratitude and reverence for Dr. Sudha Rai, my teacher and supervisor. I am indebted to her for agreeing to supervise my work, for encouraging and keeping faith in me during my periods of stress and depression, and for her highly distinguished guidance throughout the period.

I feel a deep sense of gratitude for my grandfather and parents who, despite difficulties, continued their generous support and encouragement till the very end. My thanks are due to Mr. M.C. Jain who, knowing my desire to pursue studies further, directed me to take up this challenging task.

I was able to complete this task because of the congenial environment provided by my friends — Dr. Sanskriti Raonka, Manjula Jain, Shaila Daga, Anita Singh — during my stay in the hostel at Banasthali Vidyapith. I can never forget the middle phase of my work, when, completely disheartened by the difficulties, I felt a temptation to give up the task. But I could overcome my sense of incompetence owing to the efforts made by my supervisor, my father and my friends.

I take this opportunity to thank those of my friends and relatives who helped me procure valuable material from the British Council Library, Delhi and Rajasthan University Library, Jaipur. They also encouraged me at times when I needed it most.

I acknowledge, with gratitude, the cooperation and financial assistance granted to me, in the final phase of my work, by the President, Rajasthan Textile Mills, Bhawani Mandi.

Preface

The present investigation owes its roots to a reasoned intuition based on a close reading of the plays of W.B. Yeats and T.S. Eliot that in spite of a sharp ideological antagonism between them, their common intention was to elevate and popularized poetic drama. I propose to verify through a linguistic stylistic study of their texts, how intention acquires linguistic from at levels ranging from lexical, grammatical and discoursal to the interactive speech levels. The concept of linguistic stylistics has been revolutionized during the present century. It does not simply mean the study of a literary text that pays particular attention to its language. Halliday defines the changed concept of linguistic study in the following manner :

> In talking of the linguistic study of literary texts we mean, of course, not 'the study of language' but 'the study (of the language) by the theories and methods of linguistics ... that may reasonably be called 'linguistic stylistics.[1]'

The newer explorations in the field of linguistics provide us with theories and methods that lead to more meaningful studies of literature. Nils Erik Enkvist focuses on the shift in language studies when he observes :

> Linguists are interested in all kinds of linguistic variations. And style in only one of many types of such variations. Other types are temporal. regional and social dialect, as well as Idiolect and Register.[2]

These concepts of modern linguistics will be defined in the introductory chapter. These concepts, along with certain other theories, that will be discussed in the introduction, correlate linguistic features of the literary text and variations within it with the contextual features of the text.

Such studies which establish a close alliance between language and literature, are favoured by Leo Spitzer who proceeds from the linguistic plane towards the underlining principle of the text and then proposes to make "the return trip to all the other groups of observation in order to find whether the inward from one has tentatively constructed gives an account of the whole." Spitzer believes, "the scholar will surely be able to state, after three or four of these fro-voyages, whether he has found the life giving centre, the sun of the solar system."[3]

A close scrutiny of the linguistic features reveals the true significance and meaning of a text besides providing us with concrete evidence for our initial impressions. Our intuitive response, as a consequence, may sometimes be modified. Nevertheless, the wonder or the beauty of a text will be enhanced as we find the concrete linguistic evidence for out aesthetic response.

This investigation, therefore, aims at illuminating Yeats and Eliot's poetic drama by identifying dominant linguistic features within the plays which constitute their ideological expression.

REFERENCES

1. M.A.K. Halliday, *The Linguistic Study of Literary Texts,* p. 14.
2. Nils Eric Enkvist, *Linguistic Stylistics,* p. 16.
3. Leo Spitzer, *Linguistics and Literary History,* p. 19.

Contents

Chapter - 1

Introduction : This Language Dimension

The horizons of language study have immensely expanded during the present century. Sometimes new dimensions are discovered and at other times there is a shift in focus from one aspect of language to another. The twentieth century language perspective approaches language with a different outlook compared with the traditional attitude towards it. The theories and methods of modern linguistics do not show a linear progression. But the various developments in this field are interrelated. Since our investigation proposes to look at the language dimension of the poetic drama of W.B. Yeats and T.S. Eliot from the view point born of twentieth century explorations in the field of linguistics those experiments and explorations relevant to the inquiry are briefly traced.

The traditional language studies described language in terms of 'grammar,' which in turn was a description of the eight parts of speech. The definitions of these grammatical categories were not sharp and precise. The boundaries of functions and meanings constantly mixed together. The definitions were vague and circulatory which created confusion among the scholars. Grammar was not a descriptive discipline. Grammar meant a study of correct language. Any deviation from the prescribed rules was condemned as incorrect. Their grammar was a metalanguage comprising the eight parts of speech — with sub-divisions — which they used to categories the parts of sentences in a language. Classifications became very complex. The rigidities of definitions led to an acceptance of large numbers of exceptions. Sometimes the huge number of exceptions made the rule irrelevant. Learning language meant learning grammar. Learning grammar meant learning to make a proper choice between 'shall' and 'will', 'who' and 'whom.' The puristic attitude of traditional grammarians robbed grammar of interest.

Like the history of other disciplines, the history of language study too is punctuated by revolts against established opinions. The present century shows a large number of such revolts. A number of theories have been propounded. Some of them represent a constant effort to apply the methodology of science to the study of language.

Bloomfield studied language as a science in order that it could give useful results. He excluded psychology from linguistics and used a scientific jargon. He emphatically held that generalization about language must be based on induction : "The only useful generalizations about language are inductive generalizations .... The fact that some features are, at any rate, widespread, is worthy of notice and calls for an explanation .... "[1] His approach shows a break away from the prescriptive grammar attitude towards language.

Another scholar, Ferdinand de Saussure (1857-1913), enriched the study of language with a number of useful distinctions about the nature of language. He introduced a distinction between the concepts of 'signified' and 'signifier.' 'Signified' meant the thought or the concept and its linguistic expression was called 'signifier.' He made another distinction between 'langue' and 'parole.' Langue is an abstract system of language which is a social phenomenon. Parole is the speech of an individual speaker. He made yet another distinction between 'synchronic' and 'diachronic' studies of language. Synchronic (static) study is the study at a given point of time. It is descriptive. Diachronic study shows changes over a period of time. It is historical and evolutionary. The first studies horizontal or syntagmatic relationships while the other explores vertical or paradigmatic relationships in the system of a language. The concept of syntagmatic/paradigmatic relationship can be taken out of the framework of time. Roman Jakobson develops this point in his description of poetic language. He looks at poetic language as the projecting of 'the principle of equivalence from the axis of selection into the axis of combination.'[2] Jakobson made his famous distinction between 'metonymy' and 'metaphor' on the basis of the two axes. Metonymy relates to syntagmatic plane of language. Metaphor exploits vertical or paradigmatic relationships. Jakobson's contribution lies in bringing the study of language and the study of literature close to each other : "A linguist deaf to the poetic function of language and a literary scholar indifferent to linguistic problems and unconversant with linguistic methods, are equally flagrant anachronisms."[3]

John Stephens and Ruth Waterhouse attempt to bridge the gap between the two disciplines — literature and language. The study of language, according to them, makes a 'jumping off point' for a critical approach to the literary text. Twentieth century studies in language, they think, have much "to offer the process of literary criticism, at both the conceptual and analytical levels."[4] They take the concepts of syntagmatic/paradigmatic relationship and signified/signifier relationship from Saussure and interrelate the two :

> "The signifier/signified relationship within the sign is focussed or defined or even subverted by the paradigm/syntagm relationship within which it is located."

A writer selects a particular signifier for a variety of reasons : its register, its overtones, its sound, its ability to rhyme with another already chosen, its concreteness or abstractness, and so on. The selected signifier is then further defined by its context. It is also defined by "what it is not, and partly by reason of semantic relationships or sound similarity or some other association, cultural or individual, so that a core of meaning is surrounded by a number of associations."[5]

Apart from the syntagmatic context, the paradigmatic axis too has varied possibilities that introduce the third dimension as the signifier in its paradigmatic slot directs the reader back to the signified, indeterminate as that signified may be in some respects. This is a shifting dimension. In prose, generally, the signifier is 'transparent,' or 'like a window.' "Whereas in verse cultural convention and long tradition encourage readers to perceive the signified with the signifier more consciously in mind. Even within verse, however, the relative weighing of one as against the other can minimise or maximise the gap between the two."[6]

The interaction between syntagm/paradigm and signifier/ signified is also able to "float the signifier away form the signified to which, through normal coding, it is conventionally if arbitrarily related."[7] The drifting apart between the two occurs when the context detaches the conventionally coded signified from the signifier, and leaves indeterminate the signified that the whole context seems to demand. The various concepts examined in this study by John Stephens and Ruth Waterhouse will help our investigation in exploring the way Yeats and Eliot used language in their poetic drama.

The basic tenets of Saussuream linguistics are usefully applied in the structuralist poetics. The structuralists systematised the concepts of 'langue' and 'parole'. They discovered the nature of the component signs of a text and its system that governed the use and combination of its signs. They studies the formal structures which organise a text and make possible a range of meanings.

Structuralist critics worked with the larger units of a text, its plot, characters and its style of narrative. Seturaman took the example of Vladimir Propp's 'Morphology of the Folktale' in which Propp derived the structure of a master-tale. He found that the personages of a tale were variable but their functions were constant and limited. The characters were invested with narrative significance. The narrative pattern was linear. He listed a total number of thirty— one fuctions that made the tale's action. "He distributed the functions among seven 'spheres of action' which are villain, the donor, the helper, the princess, and her father, the dispatcher, the hero and the false hero."[8] Propp derived a grammar of narrative from the deep structure of the folk-tales. His study, according to Roger Fowler, "Subordinate aspects of surface structure in favour of an investigation of some deeper, more abstract patterns which govern the inner form of a work; this form can be related to that of other works and ultimately perhaps to the general conventions of all literary discourse."[9] The concept of the patterns of the inner form of a work will be the basis of our concept of structural rhythms. The plays of Yeats and Eliot create such patterns or rhythms that have their roots in the ideologies and intentions of the writers.

Like the structuralist critics, Russian Formalists too insisted on the self-contained character of the literary work. Literature, for them, was essentially a linguistic phenomenon. They distinguished a poem as a set of contrivances superimposed on ordinary speech and looked upon rhythm as its crucial aspect. Their notion of form is strictly literary and technical. Form is an organization of various components of a text. They denounced the attempts to separate form and content. Form, for them, was not a mere outer embellishment. It was a principle, controlling and unifying the text. Form has the power to generate meaning by the manipulation of possibilities and ambiguities inherent in its verbal medium. In this respect, they are like the New Critics who derive the whole meaning from the text itself and put faith in form as a principle of integration.

Roman Jakobson extended the scope of Russian Formalism into linguistics. He was associated with Russian Formalism. He moved over to Czechoslovakia and helped shape the Prague Linguistic Circle. For the Prague linguists poetics was an integral part of semantics rather than a branch of linguisties.

The linguists of the London School took a very different view of language. The leading voice of this school was J.R. Firth. He thought of linguistics as a social science. He was primarily concerned with a contextual approach to language and making statements of meaning at all the levels of linguistic approach. Firth wanted the study of language to start with man's active participation in language. The major functions of language, for them, were lexical, morphological, syntactical and the function of context of situation. Meaning is not a hidden mental process. It is a complex of contextual relationships. Their analysis deals with texts by setting up horizontal structures and vertical systems. Social context could be analysed, classified and systematized. Then it could be used as an explicit part of linguistic analysis of language. Context of situation relates and act of speech to relevant elements of the non-speech reality as well as the other acts of speech. Any act of speech has two realms to relate to the internal context of the text and the external world. Interior relations include features of participants and their effect. The exterior world consists of everything other than the act of speech or the text under consideration. In the Firthian school the problem of classification becomes monstrous. An act of speech, or a unit of discourse may either be context free or may have innumerable contexts.

The linguists of the later generations, therefore, talked less about the context of situation. The neo-Firthian scholars constituted a separate branch of institutional linguistics. For them two concepts are important — the concept of 'register' and the concept of 'style.' Neo-Firthians like M.A.K. Halliday and McIntosh etc. proposed a set of assumptions for the study of language. One is that the language is a patterned human activity. Another assumption is that the theory of language discovers how language works. They believed that to discover the process of language function one has to work upon three levels — substance, form and context. Substance is their raw-material. Form is primarily a linguistic phenomenon. It refers to the levels of grammar and lexis. Context is tied to grammar as well as lexis. Lexis is tied to the textual features on the one hand and to the extra-textual or contextual features on the other hand. On the level of form they had a set of four fundamental categories — unit, structure, class and system. Units of grammar compose structure. Structure is the linear or syntagmatic arrangement of the elements. A class is the vertical or paradigmatic arrangement of elements of structure. Since language is patterned human activity there is a system in our language.

Halliday has tried to make the concept of system more meaningful. Language has four functions — logical, experimental, discoursal and speech function (interpersonal). These four functions constitute the four components of grammar and in every component there is a system. Halliday's descriptive linguistics takes discourse as the basic functional unit of language. Discourse is a coherent stretch of language. It is a unit larger than sentence, having a communicative function. Halliday describes any discourse under three categories : field of discourse, mode of discourse, and tenor of discourse. M.A.K. Halliday, Peter Strevens, Angus McIntosh take the three aspects of a discourse to define their concept of register.

'Field of discourse' relates to the substance of the text which is determined by the area in which the language activity operates. The area might be religion, politics, psychology, occult, journalism etc. Each field has its distinct features that influence the language. Field of discourse has a particular influence upon the lexical choice of a discourse. Literature, in this context, can be considered as one field of discourse. The register of literature can be taken as a broad category of register variation. There can be finer levels of delicacy, within a broad category, leading to classifications and sub-classifications. For example, the register of literature may have the registers of prose and poetry as its sub-classifications. The genre of poetic drama affects its lexical choice in a particular way.

The 'mode of discourse' implies a distinction between writer and spoken discourse. Within these primary modes and cutting across them there are further modes of discourse like the language of newspapers, advertising etc. "Like other dimensions of classification in linguistics, both descriptive and institutional, the classification of modes of discourse is variable in delicacy. We may first identify 'the language of literature' as a single register; but at the next step we would separate the various generes, such as prose fiction and light verse, as distinct registers within it."[10] Prose fiction belongs to the written mode whereas light verse is a written mode that is primarily to be spoken.

The third dimension of discourse analysis — the tenor of discourse — depends upon the relationship between the speaker/writer and hearer/reader. The tenor of discourse is concerned with the degree of formality in the situation. "To the extent that these affects and determine features of the language, they suggest a primary distinction into colloquial and polite .... Various more delicate cuts have been suggested such as 'casual,' 'intimate' and 'deferential'"[11] Different scales of formality or informality are marked by differences in linguistic features. The first person narrative in a novel often tends to incline the language towards the informal scale as compard to the third person narrative which is more formal.

The field, mode and tenor dimensions of discourse are, obviously, inter-related and inter-dependent. Certain fields of discourse are related more with one mode than another. Shifts in one dimension are often accompanied by shifts in other dimensions. "The formal properties of any given language event will be those associated with the intersection of the appropriate field, mode and style. A lecture on biology in a technical college, for example, will be in the scientific field, lecturing mode and polite style. more delicately in the biological field, academic lecturing mode and teacher to student style."[12]

Halliday's linguistics view language as a functional phenomenon. The function of a language differs in different situations. And language varies with its function. The name given to a variety of language according to its use is 'register.' Halliday's description of a discourse under the categories discussed above defines the concept of register.

The pragmatic or functional theory of linguistics puts emphasis upon the interactive role of language. The dynamic theory takes language as an activity in itself. J.L. Austin, Levinson and other linguists have evolved a theory of 'speech acts' in which language becomes an event. Language, here, does not simply reflect the reality. It creates its own reality. It does not take language as conveying some concepts in varying linguistic garbs. It views language as a mode of action. Speech act means verbal events or spoken action. The theory studies the dynamic role of language using a three-fold distinction. First, we recognise that an act of communication takes place, i.e., the locutionary act. Secondly, we look at the act that is performed as a result of the utterance — the illocutionary act. Thirdly, we study the particular effect an utterance has on the hearer, the bringing about of such an effect is known as perlocutionary act. The second and the third act may or may not coincide. The hearer may or may not respond in the way the speaker desires. In the case of speech acts the linguistic activity makes the whole of the relevant activity.

The speaker who performs the illocutionary act employs a number of linguistic resources — varying styles of speech like a rhetorical style, a diplomatic or sincere style, a circumlocutory or straight forward style. He selects his style as required by the context and the perlocutionary effect that he desires to bring about. Selection of a particular style implies used of other linguistic features like diction, syntax, tone, rhythm, images and symbols, in a manner appropriate for the chosen style.

The theory of speech-acts is very rewarding for the study of dramatic discourse. As quoted in Keir Elam, Richard Ohmann claims that in drama action 'rides on a train of illocutions.'[13] Different characters in a play perform speech-acts for different reasons. The style of their illocutions reflects their purpose. The failure or success of a character's illocutionary acts may reflect the characteristics of its hearer. It brings into foreground the values that a writer wants to uphold or revive in the society. If a writer wants to perform certain perlocutionary acts, i.e., to persuade his audience to accept his evaluation of experience and his system of beliefs, he needs perform repeated acts of illocution during his writing of plays. Apart from the linguistic tools available to a character he will create certain patterns of themes, characters, symbols, and echos to give a rhythm to his creation. Such structural rhythms again bring to prominence the aims and ideology of a dramatist. The various levels and aspects of speech-act there will supply us with the major tools for the interpretation of the poetic drama of Yeats and Eliot.

For a study of dramatic texts it is useful to separate the language activity of an individual from the language activity of a text and the language activity of a writer. The concept of 'idiolect' in modern linguistics becomes a significant tools for such a purpose. Idiolect refers to the whole language activity of an individual : his choice of words and his unique manner of defining certain items of vocabulary, his individual manner of pairing words, his tone and style of speech, his choice of images and symbols from a particular register of language etc. It is important in contrasting and comparing characters and bringing out the differences or similarities of values among them. It helps to separate an individual being from a social character or a stereotype personality. The ideolect of a character never fails to show whether he feels alienation from the surrounding world or feels a oneness with other characters. This concept of idiolect will be, along with the concept of register and speech-act theory, another major tools in our investigation.

Drama being a social art the concept of dialect in socio-linguistics acquires significance for our study. Modern linguistic stylistics explores the functional aspect of this category. Dialect is language according to the user. It depends upon the place of a speaker in the social hierarchy as well as upon the geographical area that he inhabits. It is a socio-geographical variety of language. Use of a particular dialect implies an emphasis upon the cultural values of a particular group in the society whose dialect is taken for the language of a text or a character in the context of drama. It is needed for the preservation of ethnic identiy. It strikes an immediate rapport with the audience who share the dialect with the characters on the stage.

The new context of language studies created in the twentieth century makes possible and rewarding a fersh look at a dramatic genre, laden with textual and socio-cultural nuances. Poetic drama pursues high socio-cultural goals. Its language and form are elevated. Poetry, being a unification of words and music, is capable of voicing the subtleties of being. Used in drama, its aim is to stir the souls of the audience. A verse playwright intends to bring about a spiritual awakening in the masses who otherwise alacken because of the monotony and drudgery of the everyday life. Only poetry can lead to an awareness of the deeper nuances of the soul. It can initiate a process of evolution leading men and women to live life more richly and meaningfully. It can serve as a medium of communication at the level of souls — such is the stated ideological intent of Yeats and Eliot.

The form of poetic drama is equally stylized or elevated. It is chiselled to suit the high-pitched drama of the inner self. Symbolic characterisation, stylized action, chorus, masks, dance, visual imagery etc. are some of the tools in the hands of a dramatist that assist him elevate the form. Dramatic and theatrical skills are combined with linguistic devices to create a drama that is 'remote spiritual and ideal', to use Yeats' phrase.

If a dramatist desires to awaken and convert to spiritual being, he needs to communicate his meaning successfully. Poetic drama aims to initiate and accelerate this process of conversion. It emerges paradoxically that to elevate, a playwright must popularize. The social dimension is an essential one for this genre of literature. Popularization is the condition prior to elevation.

Our exploration of Yeats and Eliot's poetic drama looks into the linguistic stylistic implications of this ambitious goal of a poet-plywright — which may be stated as elevation — popularization.The aim of the combined motive of elevation and popularization forms the core of the problematics of verse drama. The problem is reflected in various aspects of the dramatist's discourse. He can choose his register from various fields of discourse. To elevate he needs grand, abstract works. Whereas to fulfil the demands of communication to heterogeneous audience, he will choose his words from the field of popular language. His lexical choice will, therefore, be pulled in two directions — one towards the field of discourse that has common, simple, concrete terms and another again, towards the elevated field of discourse. The pull in apparently contrary directions will generate a tension in the vocabulary of a verse playwright. He has to face the challenge to fuse the two fields together. Being a creative writer he enjoys a privilege to shift and mix his fields of discourse. The register of prose, poetry, music, religion, the occult, psychology, science, law, etc. are equally accessible to him. Apart from shifting and mixing various registers an imaginative writer can also suggest a deep register while using a different surface register. In his later plays Eliot keeps the religious register concealed beneath the secular, modern register that he uses.

Like the field to discourse, the mode of discourse too presents a challenge to a verse playwright. Poetic drama involves a tension between written modes of discourse and spoken modes of discourse. Poetic drama, being an exalted genre of writing, implies a mode of discourse that is sublime and high. Spoken mode brings in the features of colloquial or actual conversation. A playwright needs to blend the high with the low styles of language. The written mode is elevated and formal whereas the spoken mode is informal and ordinary in its tenor and field of discourse. The possibility of shifting and mixing the features of different modes is open to a creative writer.

The tenor of discourse reflects the relationship between the characters on the stage. The pull of motives in the directions of elevation and popularization is reflected and rendered creatively in the tenor or discourse. The relationship between the characters on the stage is as much relevant to and reflected in the tenor of dialogue as is the relationship which a dramatist wants to build up between the actors and the audience. It is a powerful weapon in the hands of a dramatist with which he can manipulate audience response. He channels the sympathies of his audience in a particular direction. His ideology governs and is reflected in his choice of the direction in which he leads his audience. Soliloquies are informal and intimate in tenor and, therefore, immediately build a relationship between the actor and the audience. Shakespeare put solitoquies in the mouth of his tragic protagonists. Soliloquies reveal the speaker's alienation from his surroundings while demonstrating his yearing for communication. The choric songs, in Yeats and Eliot, that murmur secrets into the ears of the protagonist as well as the audience also perform the same kind of function. Whereas, the highly symbolic and reflective songs that they insert distance the drama and carry it to higher planers of existence. The formal tenor of discourse makes the drama 'remote spiritual and ideal' and the informal tenor creates a report between the actors and audiences.

The elevation-popularization motive generates problems for a playwright at various other levels of language. Apart from the field, mode and tenor dimensions of discourse the language of drama makes creative uses of idiolect, dialect, signifier-signified relationships, speech-acts, rhythms of the play and styles of speech. The problems of poetic drama make necessary for the playwright a creative or imaginative exploration of the above mentioned categories of linguistic stylistics. Some of these creative uses of the language dimension have been discussed while tracing the major trends in twentieth century linguistics. The present inquiry investigates the plays of Yeats and Eliot so as to discover how their language and creative uses of linguistic resources help them pursure their goals.

A survey of the major trends in drama criticism from the age of Shakespeare to the present century evinces a dearth of linguistic studies in the field of drama. Drama criticism has concentrated its focus on the traditional literary, dramatic and theatrical aspects. Dramatic and theatrical aspects are inseparably knit with the language aspect of a play. But there has been a dearth of focus on the linguistic resources, problems and explorations in poetic drama apart from the eternal controversy regarding prose and poetry that has always attracted much critical activity right from the Elizabethans to our own writers — Yeats and Eliot. Aristotle's *Poetics* sidelined the question of prose and poetry laying emphasis on plot that was the first principle of drama for him. Character, diction, thought, spectacle and song were the other elements of drama subordinated to plot. Like Aristotle the Elizabethan and Jacobean playwrights and critics were interested in the question of comedy versus tragedy. But they defied the rules prescribed by Aristotle. Shakespeare flaunted the concepts of separate genres and unities of time place and action as prescribed in *Poetics.* Shakespeare created his own standards of excellence in drama. John Fletcher justified tragicomedy as a separate genre in his *Preface to the Faithful Shepherdess.* The Elizathan, unlike Aristotle, showed much concern with the question of poetry. Sir Philip Sidney's *The Defense of Poesy* and Samuel Daniel's *A Defense of Rhyme* surprise us as we do not find any defense necessary for the significance of poetry. Though the question of poetry on the stage has never been answered finally.

Dryden and Samuel Johnson saw virtue and excellence in Shakespeare though for different reasons. Dryden found Shakespeare's abandonment of Aristotelean rules magnificient. Johnson discovered that Shakespeare held the most faithful mirror to nature in his plays. Johnson also believed that comedy came more naturally to Shakespeare than tragedy. Much of the drama criticism revolves around Shakespeare in the neo-classical age. Drama criticism,, as yet has taken drama as a literary text.

The romantic drama criticism is less overtly haunted by the giant figure of Shakespeare. The romantics take a different view of drama from the Neo-classicists :

> Unlike the neo-classicists, who wrote that theatre should delude the spectator, through veri-simililude.... Coleridge regards as the basis of dramatic illusion the audience's 'willing suspension of disbelief,' that is, belief in not what is unreal but 'a negative unreality,' a temporary willingness not to admit the reality.[14]

Coleridge's poetic faith, 'the willing suspension of disbelief,' and attention to the text anticipated modern symbolist criticism.

With the advent of Ibsen's naturalistic prose drama, drama criticism began to consider drama as theatrical performance. Shaw's criticism made drama criticism journalistic. G.B. Shaw shifted the focus of drama criticism from the question of genre and language to the question of social problems.

Unlike his countryman Shaw, Yeats opposed dialactic drama and naturalistic acting. "He favoured a theatre of passion and poetry, and he advocated acting and stage craft that had simplicity and beauty."[16] Yeats and Synge asked for and provided both reality and joy. The source of joy lay in vivid and musical idiom of rural Ireland.

The resurgence of verse drama by T.S. Eliot and Christopher Fry brought back the ancient faith in words — belief in the language of drama as the most significant part of it. The drama criticism of the twentieth century varies in its approaches from those which take a minimal to those which see it in its widest contexts. Yeats sought to establish *'the sovereignty of words'* on the stage. On the contrary the theatre of the absurd tends towards a devaluation of language. Yeats wanted to reform theatre by cultivating a stronger feeling for beautiful and appropriate language in audiences as well as writers. The theatre of the Absurd establishes a new equation with language :

> The theatre of the Absurd tends toward a radical *devaluation of language,* toward a poetry that is to emerge from the concrete and objectified images of the stage itself. The element of language still plays an important part in this conception, but what happens on the stage transcends, and often contradicts, the words spoken by the characters.[17]

In the plays of Beckett and Pinter language exists in its apparent opposite, i.e., silence. The playwrights of the absurd school often happen to communicate more meaning through a creative use of silence instead of communicating through words. They express their anguish at the absurdity of the human condition and the inadequacy of the rational approach by the open abandonment of rational devices and discussive thought. They do not trust the rational processes of language and the dramatic form. They try to achieve a unity between their basic assumptions and the form in which they express them : a unity that Yeats too strove to achieve though with different basic assumptions.

Dramatic criticism owes its development to the hybrid nature of drama — drama as text in apposition with drama as performance. With the evolution of new theatrical techniques and advance in technology drama criticism has become theatre oriented.

Criticism in the olden times had concentrated its focus on drama *as literary text.* The language of drama had been studied with a *traditional approach towards* language that studied the aesthetic aspect of language.

The present investigation, though taking the traditional approach towards drama — drama as text, intends to study the language of Yeats' and Eliot's drama with categories opened up by modern linguistics. These studies view language as communication, relating it to its social context. The concepts of register, dialect, idiolect, speech — acts, styles of speech are aspects of language in use. By a combination of lexical varieties, language styles and genres drama emerges as a dynamic discourse with the help of which Yeats and Eliot intended to educate as well as entertain their audiences.

Their intention to revive poetic drama is a blending of cultural motive with the linguistic motive. The two motives are interdependent and gain authenticity from each other. To educate their audiences in the spiritual awakening they needed poetry and the poetry in their drama finds backing from their stated cultural goal. Only poetry they felt, could realize their cultural motive. Their primacy to words along with the advances in the language studies during the present century stimulated and guided the shape of the present study which claims to fill up the space left by critics even after a large number of studies upon the 'two Greats — W.B. Yeats and T.S. Eliot.

REFERENCES

1. Bloomfield, *Language*, p. 20.
2. J. Sebeok, ed., *Style in Language*, p. 358.
3. *Ibid.*, p. 358.
4. John Stephens and Ruth Waterhouse, *Literature, Language and Change : From Chaucer to the Present*, p. 6.
5. *Ibid.*, pp. 13-14.
6. *Ibid.*, p. 16.
7. *Ibid.*, p. 17.
8. V.S. Seturaman, *Contemporary Criticism*, p. 19.
9. Roger Fowler, ed., *Style and Structure in Literature*, p. 11.
10. M.A.K. Hathday, Peter Strevens, Angus McIntosh, *The Linguistic Science and Language Teaching*, p. 12.
11. *Ibid.*, pp. 92-93.
12. *Ibid.*, p. 93.
13. Keir Elam, *Shakespeare's Universe of discourse*, p. 7.

    Elam studies the comedies of Shakespeare and its language consciousness. He finds an active and self-advertising presence of language in his comedies. Through the speech-act theory Keir Elam proves that language is a dynamic protagonist in Shakespeare's comedies.
14. Bernard F. Dukore, *Dramatic Theory and Practice : Greeks to Grotowski*, p. 577.
15. *Ibid.*, p. 579.
16. *Ibid.*
17. *Ibid.*, p. 672.

Chapter Two

Poetic Drama : Intention and Ideology

Poetic drama is a highly challenging genre of creative writing. Men of genius in every age aspired to achieve distinction in the field of poetic drama. Shakespeare won universal fame and the highest distinction as a verse playwright. The wealth of poetic drama inherited from him is the pride of English language and literature. After the age of Shakespeare the tradition of poetic drama had seen a deterioration. The playwright invariably happened to produce plays that poorly imitated Shakespeare and hence failed to make a mark in the theatre. The history of drama reveals that for the three consecutive centuries following Shakespeare poetic drama was in the decline. The age of Pope and Dryden was primarily an age of prose and satire. Satiric verse, prose and comedies were the dominant forms of writing. Prose replaced poetry in the theatre. Comedy was taken seriously by the genius of this age.

The writers in the Romantic age did make attempts to write verse plays. But their enthusiasm for the lyrical and the emotional resulted in the creation of plays that were either sentimental or melodramatic. Wordsworth's play, *The Borderers,* did not succeed as it was found to be melodramatic by the theatre managers, though his friend Coleridge praised it very highly for 'the profound touches of the human heart.' Coleridge's play *Zapolya* too was not found stage- worthy. These writers tended to create characters that were types rather than individuals. They put abstract qualities in the form of characters. They could not combine the modes of prose and poetry effectively. Another inherent defect in the drama of this period was its over literal stage presentation that left no room for symbols or imagery. The verse dramatist of this period faced a struggle against the popular theatre which was catering to the demands for spectacle and pantomime.

In the Victorian era melodrama satisfied the need for spectacle and sensation :

> Melodrama with its substitution of sensation for emotion, situation for structure, and spectacle for nearly every thing had taken the place of tragedy.[1]

A deterioration in public taste has set in. It disabled the audience to appreciate finer works. Romantics had left no living theatre though the impulse to writer plays in verse was strong in them. Since Victorians did not inherit a theatre they did not attempt to write drama.

After 1860, a number of playwrights heralded a realistic school of drama. They aimed at writing plays close to real life in theme and in style. This group of writers discarded romantic sentimantality and Victorian melodrama. T.W. Robertson was a pioneer in this field. He, along with H.A. Jones and A.W. Pinero rejected poetry in order to relate the language of their characters to the spoken language of their time. Their characters were deliberately stripped of all heroic qualities so that they could look like people in their social roles. This movement gained momentum with the entrance of Henrik Ibsen on the theatrical scene. His realistic social plays in prose carried the goal of realism still further. Realism became the ultimate goal to be pursued. But very soon this extremity of realism led to a kind of nostalgic desire among poets to revive poetic drama.

Wilfred Wilson Gibson, Lescelles Abercrombie and John Drinkwater occupy a middle position between realistic plays in prose and symbolic poetic drama of the twentieth century. They took their settings from the realistic prose plays whereas their style looked forward to the poetic drama of the following decades. They employed a new dialect and new social material : Gibson's *Krindlesyke* is flavoured with words of a northern dialect. They wanted to partake the corporate flavour of the movement. Their endeavour was to bring poetry close to life. Abercrombie pointed out that poety had a quality of its own. He wanted poetry to be based on the spoken word. He echoes J.M. Synge who employed the real language of the people of Aran islands which was rich in poetry. His prose plays were successfully staged in Ireland. John Drinkwater was a practical man of theatre. He achieved success by writing prose plays. These playwrights show an enthusiasm for poetry though they wrote in prose for theatrical reasons. Like their contemporaries in Ireland they discovered a refreshing liveliness in the depiction of simple in their own language. But this movement remained outside the main stream drama. In the mainstream flew the giant figure of G.B. Shaw along with Granville Barker and William Archer :

> The existing dramatic tradition is that in which Cernard Shaw, Granville Barker and William Archer triumphed over a decayed 'poetic' tradition diversely represented by Irving, Gordon Craig and Celtic Twilight. The intellectual content has been gradually swallowed up by an increasing sentimentalism, but the form remains both for the playwright and the actor. Naturalness in the sense of a photographic realism, insensibility to the qualities of the spoken word, the reduction of the visual to insignificance — these are the aspects of the form by which the drama was reduced to the service of a purpose foreign to it.[2]

When poetic drama was rejuvenated in the twentieth century W.B. Yeats made a careful study of the causes that led to a deterioration in the quality of theatrical production and a decline of poetic drama :

> When the first day of the drama has passed by actors found that an always large number of people were more easily moved through the eyes than through the ears. The emotion that comes with the music of words is exhausting emotion, and few people like exhausting emotions : and therefore actors began to speak as if they were reading something out of the newspaper. They forgot the noble art of oratory and gave all their thought to the poor art of acting .... As audiences and actors chang managers learned to substitute meretricious landscapes, printed upon wooc and canvas, for the description of poetry, until the painted scenery became as important as the story. It needed some imagination, some gift for

> day-dreams, to see the horses and the fields and the flowers of Colonus as one listened to the elders gathering about Oedipus ....; but it needed no imagination to admire a painting by somebody who understands how to show everything to the most hurried glance....[3].

Yeats perceived that audiences, producers and playwrights were equally responsible for bringing about the decline of poetic drama. He acknowledges the powers of poetic drama that involves an imaginative participation from its audience.

Yeats and Eliot, along with Sturge Moore, Masefield, Binyon and Bottomley initiated as war against the realistic school of Ibsen and Galesworthy and Shaw who wrote social problem plays in prose. Masefield's Garden Theatre, Oxford was the Centre of activities where the group of playwrights including Bottomley, Sturge Moore, Binyon carried their experiments with various techniques and traditions of poetic drama. Like Yeats this group of playswrights shows an enthusiasm for Japanese Noh drama. And like Eliot they preferred religious themes. Bottomley takes various aspects of Scottish life and its legends for his plays. He made a limited use of Noh techniques. He used songs from behind the curtain. This device was intended to demonstrate the value of poetry to the audience. Yeats dared to move one step ahead having songs on the stage. Bottomley used choric songs to intensify the dramatic excitement. Here he was followed by T.S. Eliot. Lawrence Binyon showed an interest in the spoken poetry. He wrote plays for the recitation of his poetry on the stage. Yeats shows a similar desire in his poetic plays. Sturge Moore was interested in biblical and classical themes for his symbolic drama. He was introduced to the Noh theatre by W.B. Yeats. Moore's plays could be heard from behind the curtain. He took great pains to demonstrate the importance of poetry on the stage. Masefield combined the Noh techniques with the conventions of Greek and Elizabethan tragedy. He wanted to rekindle the imagination of the audience through poetic drama.

W.B. Yeats continued and intensified the struggle to win back the right place of poetry in the theatre. He wanted to lead his age back to a reality different from the reality depicted in the drama of his predecessors — the reality that reveals itself in poetic thought as opposed to the photographic realism of Ibsen type. Poetry can penetrate into the deeper significance of surface reality. He guarded against the merely decorative verses :

> It is not difficult to construct a fairly vigorous verse play, and then ... to decorate it and encumber it with poetry. But a play of that kind will never move us poetically, because it does not uncover, as it were, the high, intellectual delicately organised soul of men, and of an action, that may not speak aloud if it does not speak in verse.[4]

Poetry, according to Yeats, is essential for drama if it aims at voicing the soul. Drama must be a dialogue of the soul. Yeats also desired all his poetry to be spoken on the stage. The voices of the soul should stir the soul in other people. The communication between the author and the audience was to take place at the level of soul.

Part of the superiority of poetry lay in the music of words that could be realised only when sung aloud. Yeats was always conscious of the appeal of the spoken words. Yeats tried "to clear out of poetry every phrase written for the eye, and bring all back to syntax that is for the ear alone."[5]

Yeats liked a poem spoken with 'a sense of its rhythm' and 'a respect for its meaning.' He hated any unnatural prolonging of vowel sounds in a word which "did not give it its exact place and weight in the rhythm."[6] He had the romantic writer's love of oral ballad poetry. Wordsworth was attracted to ballad because of its closeness to life. Yeats liked it for its oral tradition and also for its closeness to life. His fascination with the spoken work was so over-powering that he subordinated other elements of drama to the words. He wanted "to get rid of irrelevant movement — the stage must become still that words might keep all their vividness — and I wanted vivid words."[7]

Yeats wanted the vividness and the musicality of the spoken words to carry the whole burden of meaning. Action an stylization provided the context necessary for such words. In this context the study of Yeats' langugae acquires a special significance.

The spoken word was to be taken from the language of the people whose life a play calims to depict. Here again Yeats shows his romantic bent of mind. Wordsworth's *Preface to Lyrical Ballads,* that is the pivot of romantic aesthetics, puts its faith in the language of peasants which is simple and natural. Yeats sent J.W. Synge to the Aran Islands advising him to learn the dialect of Aran Islands and use it in his drama.

> The idiom of the Irish speaking people of the west is the only good English spoken by any large number of Irish people today, and we must found good literature on a living speech, seeing the difference between dead and living words, between words that meant something years ago and words that have the only thing that gives literary quality - personality, the breath of men's mouth.[8]

Besides having faith in the living language, Yeats also believed in the richness and superiority of Irish dialect and its accents. A rehabilitation of Irish dialect and accents in the theatre had the potential to serve the aim of cultural integration that was one of Yeats' dominant preoccupations and intentions as a verse dramatist. In his essay on Yeats, Eliot recognised that Yeats "cared, I think, more for the theater as an organ for the expression of the consciousness of a people than as a means to his own fame or achievement."[9]

To help the cultural unification of Ireland, Yeats dramatised Irish myths and legends in his plays. He aimed at "awakening heroic passions dormant in racial memory." By the use of significant character allusions Yeats wished to "transmute the topical into archetypal."[10] The image of a hero who seems but is not defeated, is deep rooted in the Celtic soil. Cuchulain is one of the major legendary heroes. Parnell, Maud Gonne and other political revolutionaries of his time become the contemporary equivalents of the legendary hero. Maud Gonne relates to another legendary figure, Countess Cathleen who sells her soul to the demon merchants in order to retrieve the souls of her famine-stricken people.

Irishness in Yeats is more than Irish accents, legends and character allusions. It means a belief in the culture that regards the world of imagination as valid as reality and the concrete world. This faith gives validity to the world of his dreams :

> I did not believe with my intellect that you could be carrid away body and soul, but I believed with my emotion and the belief of the country people made that easy.[11]

For Yeats Irish meant imaginative and spiritual as opposed to scientific and rational. He believed, like Romantics, in the emotional dimension of human beings : "To me it is a fundamental defect in modern art that it too much provokes thought, classical art engenders feeling,"[12] he said to Auden. For Yeats, truly romantic is truly classical. He expressed his faith in emotions and passions more than once :

> I cannot descover truth by logic unless that logical serve passing.... The passionless reasoners are pariah dogs and devour the dead symbols.[13]

Yeats valued the free play of passion and instinct preserved in aristocracy. Modern materialism seemed to turn all instinct into inert uniformity which was repugnant to Yeats. He had an abhorrence for the men of intellect and mere opinions. He found natural vitality combined with civilized ease in aristocracy. By aristocratic he meant the proud, the heroic mind and a resentment towards the cheap and the ill-made. It is important to note, here, that Yeats recognised the virtues of a living language and the language of conuntry people. Here, he exalts the virtues of the aristocratic mind and style. The 'multitude' and the 'few' both have their virtues. The conflict is manifest in the plays of Yeats. The ways it is reflected in the shifts of motive and changes in language style will be discussed later on in the study of plays.

Yeats created an aristocratic theatre for a handful of people while he was at the apex of his career. The display of anger by the crowd at the performance of Synge's *The Playboy of Western World* and at his own *The Countess Cathleen* confirmed Yeats' belief in the philistinism of the mob. He established Irish Literary Theatre as a workshop for his own ideas. He designed it so that "the right people may escape the stupefying memory of the theatre of commerce which clings even to them. "He declared that "our plays will be for most part remote spiritual and ideal."[14] In this theatre he carried out his experiments with the techniques of Noh drama with its austere stylization and remoteness from life. He pushed his dramatic techniques and language more and more towards poetry and stylization.

It is significant that such a champion of coterie-drama should demonstrate a desire for larger audience in the later phase of his career as a dramatist. Like other playwrights, Yeats too could not resist, for long, a craving to reach out to larger segments of society. He increasingly felf dissatisfied with his ideal of drawing room audience and a theatre for 'the few.' He acknowledged the popularistic needs of drama that could not remain in the aristocratic mould of Noh for ever. He made efforts to integrate the popularization motive with the elevation motive.

The realization that drama is essentially a public art and popularization its necessary condition came late to Yeats. Eliot knew it from the beginning of his carreer as verse dramatist. To achieve the aim of popularization both the playwrights tried to fashion a new verse from that will be based on the idiom of actual conversation. Since Yeats had his faith in Irishness and the past of his nation he knew that his theatre did not exist in London's commercial West End. He created an Irish Theatre in Dublin. Whereas Eliot imitated and followed the conventions of West End comedy in the middle and later phases of his career. The two dramatists created their respective forms of new verse. For the roots of his verse Yeats relied on the roots of Irish language — its heroic past. Eliot, quite differently, modernized his verse rhythm and dialogues by imitating actual drawing room conversation and its speech rhythms. They aimed at the revival of poetic drama but it was to be a different kind of drama, written in new verse form.

Eliot too, like Yeats, objected to the aims and practices of realistic drama. In his essay of Elizabethan dramatists he says :

> The great vice of English drama from Kyd to Glasworthy has been that its aim of realism was unlimited.... It is essential that a work of art should be self-consistent, that an artist should consciously or unconsciously draw a circle beyond which he does not trespass. On the one hand actual life is always the material, and on the other hand an abstraction from actual life is a necessary condition to the creation of a work of art.[15]

A balance of abstractoin from and closeness to life is manifest in the language. The language shows a vacillation from the world of supernatural or religion to the real drawing room. It was necessary to compete with the prevailing theatre, according to Eliot :

> If the poetic drama is to reconquer its place, it must, in my opinicn, enter into overt competition with prose drama.... What we have to do is to dring poetry into the world in which the audience lives and to which it returns when it leaves the theatre : not to transport the autience into some imaginary world totally unlike its own, an unreal world in which poetry is tolerated.[16]

Eliot once remarked that 'fine art is the refinement, not the anti-thesis of popular art.' He even suggested taking a popular form and then, doing the refinement :

> Parhaps the majority of attempts to confect a poetic drama have begun at the wrong end. They have aimed at the small public which wants poetry.... Our problem should be to take a form of entertainment, and subject it to the process which would leave it a form of art. Perhaps the music hall comedian is the best material....[17]

Eliot, to revive poetic drama, could go to the extent of taking the language and techniques of music hall comedy as the beginning point. But as a perfected form he knew that poety was essential, especially to give expression to his religious world-view :

> It seems to me that beyond the nameable classifiable emotions and motives of our conscious life when directed towards action — the part of life which prose drama is wholly adequate to express — there is a fringe of indefinite extent, of feeling which we can detect. so to speak. out of the corner of the eye and can never completely focus, of feeling which we are only aware in a kind of temporary detachment from action .... This peculiar range of sensibility can be expressed by dramatic poetry, in its moments of greatest intensity.... I have before my eyes a mirage of perfection of poetic drama, which would be a design of human action and of words, such as to present at once the aspects of dramatic and of musical order.[18]

Music or rhythm of words in poetry is another reason for bringing it back to drama. The rhythms in poetry could connect with rhythms latent in human system. Rhythm, also, brings about an integration of various elements and levels of meaning in drama. It gives coherence to the parts.

The form of verse that could evoke an excitement which is needed from poetry could not be the Shakespearean verse form. Shakespearean blank verse and any echo of it was bound to fail on the twentieth century ear. Eliot realized the requirement of new metrics and new rhythms. The posibilities of blank verse as a medium of drama were exhausted. He worked cautiously to avoid any echo of Shakespeare. Shakespearean rhythms had grown remote from modern speech. A different system of versification was needed to revive poetic drama.

Yeats and Eliot felt the need for a revival of poetic drama not only for literary and aesthetic reasons but to pursue various social, cultural, religious and spiritual objectives. Their respective ideologies moulded their objectives. The language of their poetic drama is governed by their aims and ideologies and, in turn, reflects differences and similarities between the two.

"The language of Eliot's poems does not simply 'reflect' changes in his 'philosophy' but offers its own evidence about what that change amounted to,"[19] observed Graham Martin while commenting upon Eliot's conversion and declaration of Anglo-Catholicism as his religion, in 1927. Language does not simply express the established aims and ideologies but provides us with evidence for the true insights into their real selves and motives. The claims of the author himself as well as the findings of his critics may prove deceptive but his language will never fail to betray the truth.

The language of W.B. Yeats and T.S. Eliot can be approached to learn about the intellectual, emotional, imaginative and spiritual make-up of their selves. The various dimensions of their respective beings are the crucial factors in discovering their intentions as well as the depicting their motives. As already pointed out in Chapter One, their basic aim was to revive the language of poetry in the theatre. After Shakespeare either there was no poetic drama or it was not popular. They tried to write popular poetic drama. They desired to see their muses will established and acclaimed in the theatre.

Poetic drama does not. of itself, imply an immediate appeal to the audience. The history of poetic drama is a witness to the truth that excepting Shakespeare, poetic elevation and popularization necessary for drama are like two poles. They do not seem to go together. A playwright needs to fuse the poles which is a challenging task. The pulls in the opposite directions generate a peculiar tension in the framework of a drama. Our investigation will discover the features of language in the poetic drama of Yeats and Eliot that are employed by them to hold the whole dramatic structure together which might otherwise collapse under the pulls from different directions. The two men of genius of our age that Yeats and Eliot are, they are as much different in their linguistic experimentation as they diverge in their aims and ideologies.

Eliot believed that 'poetry is not a turning loose of emotion, but an escape from emotion, it is not the expression of personality, but an escape from personality.'[20] His distrust of the emotional dimension in human nature leads him to a deep dislike of the romantic writers. He found them ego-centric. Wordsworth was not a very pleasing person; Shelley was too ego-centric and abused poetry; Bynon had a defective sensibility; Goethe was no success; Lawrence's spiritual vision was sick. For Eliot, Dryden established the real tradition; Pope and Johnson were good poets and critics; Racine was a poet of high stature. He saw virtue in neo-classical and metaphysical writers. Donne has Eliot's highest approval for the 'sensuous apprehension of thought' that he was capable of.

Eliot thought that looking into the heart was not 'looking deep enough'. "One must look into the cerebral cortex, the nervous system, and the digestive tracts."[21] According to Eliot the creative activity consisted of an amalgamation of disjointed experiences like "the noise of the type-writers and the smell of cooling."[22] Writing, thus, is an act of intellect for Eliot. It must be an objective process. The creed of romantics — their subjectivity, their faith in emotions — is opposed to Eliot's intellectual and objective outlook.

When Eliot declared himself to be a classicist in literature he also declared him to be a Catholic in religion. He became a member of the English Catholic Church in 1927. The language and the images of his post — 1927 poetry too were altered. "From an initial complex weave of meaning one of two strands have been teased out. His images were, as if, 'baptised.' His language shows changes of attitude — a kind of disembodying, and withdrawing of the experience, a greater generality, and creation of mystery."[23]

Eliot felt the necessity for religion to give a sense of order to life. He had a strong sense of chaos prevailing in the world. There had been two world wars. *The Waste Land* became his representative poem depicting the sense of waste, barrenness and disorderliness as a consequence of the devastating World Wars. Religion, for Eliot, endows a sense of meaning to the otherwise meaningless existence and gives an order and unity to the disintegration in the world. He wanted to propogate his religious ethos through his poetic drama. He wrote to Martin Brown :

> In the theatre I feel then one wants a Christian mentality to permeate the theatre, to affect it and to influence audiences who might be obdurate to plays of a directly religious appeal. He didn't want to seem anti-secular. He knew that if his drama was "to be heard in the roar of London's secular entertainment, it must wear the uniform of its time and seem secular too....[24]

Eliot was against secular ideals. He felt that the whole of the contemporary literature was corrupted by secularism. It did not understand the primacy of the supernatural over the natural life. Eliot desired to convince his audience of the superiority of the supernatural. In the half-glimpsed vision of the supernatural — visible only 'out of the corner of the eye' — value and permanence are to be found. The secular world is unreal, worthless. But it is real enough to enforce its trivial demands. The idiom of Eliot's drama that affirms the reality of this world also robs it of its value. It does exist but it is divested of meaning and value unless it communes with the realm of the meaningful, the supernatural. The secular images are, therefore, deflated or undercut by the idiom, syntax and tone of his language.

The polarization of experience, character and language is between religious and secular. One group of characters in his drama is spiritually awakened, other characters are immune to this reality. The action of the drama relates to the soul of his protagonist who shows an awareness of the higher reality. The inner action needs a greater delicacy of language for its enactment. It elevates the drama to a higher level. It calls for "a heightened excitement of language, a conversation strengthened to take more than usual strain of feeling; though it should never abandon the rhythms and idiom of normal interchange, the feeling that the characters were in genuine spontaneous talk, yet it must be an empowered way of talking."[25] The play intends to disturb and excite us with what is mysterious in the familiar. It is to show us that the world of the drawing room is only one step away from the wilderness. "The language of the drawing room must therefore be ready for the extension of experience."[26]

But the precise nature of the spiritual experience eludes expression. The rational language fails to record it. It amounts to a riddling, jumble like quality of paradoxical statements. It is a measure of the intensity of such experience that it can only be suggested. Harry, in *The Family Renuion,* declares :

> I talk in general terms
> Because the particular has no language.

The particular is unique, hence, inexpressible in the language of ordinary use. The exalted, suggestive language of the first two plays — *Murder in the Cathedral* and *The Family Reunion* — is gradually brought down to bring it close to the actual drawing room dialogues.

Eliot declared that he would bring the rhythms of his dialogues close to contemporary speech rhythms. The rules of stress and caesura were to be made flexible to match the infinite variety of living speech-rhythms. His characters were supposed to speak the lines simply the way they fell, in the natural cadence that gave the fullest meaning. Imagery and diction were the tools of elevation of the drama to the higher plane whereas a desire for popularization led him to use living speech rhythms. The symbolic, poetic language of the plays of his early phase is given up, in the later phase, in favour of a non-poetic simplicity of language. The emphasis of living language and a desire for popularization in the later phase bring Eliot close to Yeats in his dramatic enterprises which are otherwise very different, in their ideology for example :

> In modern poetry Yeats and Eliot stand at opposite poles. For while both see life as incomplete, Eliot puts his faith in spiritual perfection, the ultimate conversion of sense to spirit. Yeats, on the other hand, stands with Michaelangelo for 'profane perfection of mankind,' in which sense and spirit are fully and harmoniously exploited and 'body is not bruised to pleasure soul.' So strongly does he hold this view that he projects sensuality into heaven to keep it from being ethereal and abstract. He presents this faith with such power and richness that Eliot's religion, in spite of its honesty and loftiness, is pale and infertile in comparison.[27]

Eliot is religious, Yeats secular. Eliot chose to be a classicist while Yeats declared that he was one of the last romantics. Eliot's religion involves an annihilation of the individual. His ideal is a complete merging of the will of the individual into the will of God. Yeats enhances the uniqueness of an individual. Eliot tends to be defeatist — calls the existence on this side of the grave worthless. Yeats is heroic. and his faith in gaiety stands intact even in the face of final tragedy — 'Hamlet and Lear are gay.'

Eliot puts his faith in the world beyond the boundaries of visible existence. Yeats wants to have a vigorous, joyous existence. Conflict, the vigour of life, is a positive virtue. His ideal is joyous energy — 'gaity transfiguring all.'

His outlook has the roots of drama in it. It is a proper soil where poetry can blossom. Conflict, energy, joy are the very essence of drama and poetry. Yeats believed that all the gains of men came from conflict with his opposite self. Every human being assumes a mask of its anti-self to struggle with. Out of a 'quarrel with ourselves'[28] we create poetry. The quarrel has to be set off and pursued deliberately. Conflict begins out of what is difficult. Difficult again is a positive virtue. He had a fascination of whatever was difficult because it makes drama and also because "only the greatest obstacle that can be contemplated without despair arouses the will to full intensity."[29] Whatever comes easily defeats our energy, humiliates our imagination. Joyous life is dynamic, it involves the whole being. He valued an intense, spontaneous and passionate life. Whereas, Eliot was for a disciplined, rational life. Yeats' hero is dynamic, theatrical. His idiom is power and will. Yeats believed in 'passionate Syntax,' vigorous language. Vigour of thought has to match with the vigour of expression.

Eliot's search for truth led him towards religion. Yeats' mould of mind directed him to seek for truth in occult practices, theosophical society, automatic writing etc. As a consequence the language of Yeats' drama abounds in symbols from these fields of knowledge : interpenetrating cones, phases of the moon, the tree of life, the golden bird, the hawk, the great clock tower, the heron etc. The mystic and occult thoughts form the skeleton of his drama.

Symbolic form of drama was his own choice. When he wanted to deviate from the Ibsenite-Shawian movement of realistic drama, Yeats had two alternatives before him. One was to cut under it and record the peasant culture which provided living language and simple human responses. Yeats directed J.M. Synge and Laday Gregory into this direction. For himself he knew that he was not competent to write such a drama. He chose the second path to rise above the realistic drama and create plays for small drawing-room audience of high intellectual and imaginative kind. It was to be a drama of symbol and myth with a sense of style and stylized action. This form of drama implied a remoteness for everyday life. The quality of remoteness lent strength to it. It was to be an elevated form.

Even such a remote and elevated drama gained contemporary relevance as the myths and legends of Irish life were depicted in it. Yeats' Ireland was struggling for its freedom. The movement gained momentum under the dynamic leadership of Parnell and Maud Gonne. Yeats could not remain a disinterested onlooker. Yeats, a man of dreams was called upon to become a man of action. Yeats was fascinated by the energy and beauty of Maud Gonne — a political revolutionary. He put on a mask of a man of action and set the conflict off. The conflict between dreams and responsibilities marks some of Yeats' plays.

Yeats had been a senator and had a reverence for the noble art of oratory. He depicted the legends of Ireland with a patriotic fervour and established a correspondence between the old legends and contemporary heroes. He did not hesitate to reshape or change the ancient myths. Myths were, for Yeats, archetypal symbols of eternal pursuits and fulfilment. Yeats believed in the collective unconscious of Jung. It was an ocean of images and symbols which are instinctual and not accessible to consciousness. They are the archetypal elements of all fantasies and dreams of men. The essential nature of man strives to realise itself in myths. Myths and legends multiply and enrich the resources of language making it more capable express deep-rooted impulses of man.

For Jung myth-making is a fundamental human impulse. There is a persistence of myths in literature. He proposes that poets should become myth-makers engaged in a communal enterprise. And then the ancient mythologies would find a correlative in modern life. Yeats designed his own myths in *A Vision*. He developed his system of thoughts into a personal mythology. It was to serve for the expression of the consciousness of a race. At this place, Yeats shows an influence of Blake. Blake regarded myths as the inner structure of all human history. Yeats also believed in history as a pattern of myths and tried to evoke it in his poetic drama. The language of his poetic drama attains additional layers of depth and becomes highly symbolical and connotative. It often eludes the rational processes of analysis :

> The form of sincere poetry, unlike the form of the popular poetry, may indeed be sometimes obscure, or ungrammatical as in some of the best of the *Songs of Innocence and Experience,* but it must have the perfections that escape/analyses, the subtleties that have a new meaning everyday, and it must have all this whether it be but a little song made out of the dreams of one poet and of a hundred generations whose hands were never weary of the sword.[30]

Yeats had a thorough awareness of these powers of symbolic poetry. His plays are highly symbolic till the very end of his career, though the elevated language and the stylisation of his Noh inspired drama were afterwards simplified to a large extent. A craving for large audience could not be suppressed for long. Yeats used simpler and popular forms of versification — like ballad forms — and lessened the element of mystery in the later phase. He tried to bring poetry closer to normal, everyday conversation. But, unlike Eliot, he did not want to the extent of de-poeticizing his poetry :

> I planned to write short lyrics or poetic drama where every speech would be short and concentrated, knit by dramatic tension .... I tried to make the language of poetry coincide with that of passionate, normal speech. "Again he wanted" a powerful and passionate syntax, and a complete, coincidence between period and stanza.[31]

The subsequent analyses of the plays will attempt to find language evidence of the realization of the aims and ideologies of the playwrights, as declared by them. As already pointed out, their language, not their theories, are the safer guides to understand their real intentions and beliefs.

REFERENCES :

1. Una Ellis Fermor, *The Irish Dramatic Movement,* p. 3.
2. A. Desmond Hawkins, "The Poet in the Theatre." *The Criterion,* XIV, LN (Oct. 1934), p.31.
3. W.B. Yeats, *Essays and Introductions*, p. 165.
4. *Ibid.*, p. 523.
5. *Ibid.*, p. 529.
6. *Ibid.*, p. 14.
7. *Ibid.*, p. 527.
8. W.B. Yeats, 'Samhain 1902', *Plays and Controversies,* p. 29.
9. John Hayward, ed., *T.S. Eliot : Selected Prose,* p. 199.
10. W.A. Armstrong, Intro. 'Irish Dramatic Movement', *Classic Irish Drama*, p.5.
11. W.B. Yeats, *Autobiographies,* p. 96.
12. John Stallworthy ed., *Yeats Last Poems,* p.49.
13. W.B. Yeats, *Explorations*, p. 302.
14. W.B. Yeats, *Essays and Introductions,* p.165.
15. T.S. Eliot, *Selected Essays,* p. 93.
16. T.S. Eliot, *The Sacred Wood,* p. 70.
17. *Ibid.*, p. 71.

18. T.S. Eliot, *Poetry and Drama,* p. 15.
19. Graham Martin, ed., *Eliot in Perspective,* p. 112.
20. T.S. Eliot, *Selected Essays,* p. 21.
21. *Ibid.*, p. 290.
22. *Ibid.*, p. 287.
23. Graham Martin, ed., *Eliot in Perspective,* p. 115.
24. Neville Coghill, Intro. *The Family Reunion,* p. 16.
25. *Ibid.*, p. 14.
26. *Ibid.*
27. Richard Ellmann, *The Identity of Yeats*. p. 246.
28. W.B. Yeats. *Mythologies,* p. 331.
29. W.B. Yeats, *Autobiographies,* p. 195.
30. W.B. Yeats, 'Symbol as Revelation,' *The Modern Tradition,* p. 273.
31. W.B. Yeats, *Essays and Introductions,* pp. 523-24.

Chapter - 3

The Bursting Pod : The Plays of W.B. Yeats

And I would have all know that when all falls
In ruin, poetry calls out in joy,
Being the scattering hand, the bursting pod,
The victim's joy among the holy flame,
God's laughter at the shattering of the world.

(The King's Threshold)

The present interpretation of Yeats' poetic drama correlates his aims and ideology — as discussed in the second chapter — with the features of his language experimentation. We will highlight those aspects of his language which foreground certain patterns of his theatrical and dramatic skills that relate to his intention and ethos. Our scrutiny will discover evidence for his secular or romantic or pagan outlook, his belief in the cultural superiority of Ireland, his debunking of the rational or intellectual approach towards life, his belief in the oneness of human and transhuman planes of existence, at various levels of his language use. The evidence sifts the text at the interactive level in the success and failure of various speech acts; at the semantic level in the concentration of his vocabulary in certain polarization of registers, heroic and mundane for example; at the syntactic level in various styles of speech and versification; at the lexical level in the use of certain signifiers in an unconventional manner and in various other ways that he explores the levels of language. We also notice how changes in his attitude towards the elevation popularization motive bring about newer experimentations in language and dramatic devices. How his disillusionment with the popular theatre and revelation of the phitistinism of the Irish masses pushes him towards the Noh influenced dance drama, for a small audience. In what ways the 'unpopular' theatre or drama for 'the few' affects his linguistic explorations and how his returning back to the popularization pole leads him to an ideal fusion of various elements of his drama, finally paving the way to the creation of a drama for 'the multitude' well as for 'the few.' His career as a playwrig' t reveals a pattern similar to that of a widening — contrac' . – and a further widening of the gyres. Ultimately he achieves ; .lance, widening both the gyress — that of elevation as well as ^f popularization.

THE COUNTESS CATHLEEN

Yeats selects one of the popular Irish tales for his dramatization in *The countess Cathleen* which represents his first attempt at dramatic writing. Yeats chooses the Cathleen legend for another reason also. Since it was the beginning of his career as a verse dramatist Yeats felt safe taking a Christian heroine as his protagonist. He knew that his esoteric principles would take time to become acceptable to the people of Ireland. The Cathleen legend had the advantages of being popular as it was based on a simple religious outlook towards life.

The famine in the country of the Countess compelled her people to sell their souls to demon merchants who gave money to those who transacted with them, money that kept the bodies away from starvation and death. Death seems more horrible to the simple, innocent peasants who can't imagine the sufferings that result from damnation of the soul. The soul of the Countess, being pure, innocent and angelic, is the most precious item which the demon merchants would buy at whatever price she offers. She realises her responsibility towards her people and decides to bargain her soul for the salvation of the suffering masses. She takes the path of suffering and salvation as Christ did centuries ago. The souls of her people are retrieved. Her soul too gets the reward it deserved. She enters the gates of heaven. Angels defeat the demons and win her soul for heaven.

The play is intense and symbolic in action as it is rich in language. The elements of drama and the elements of poetry exist separately. Yeats either did not try or could not achieve the fusion of the two elements. Aleel, the poet, is the major source of elevated poetic language. The major action of the play is enacted by others.

Aleel, the poet musician is given the task of keeping Cathleen's thoughts sway from the miseries of her people. He tries to dissuade her from her chosen path of self sacrifice. His language is his action :

> Aleel : I have come to bid you leave this castle and fly
> Out of these woods
>
> -----
>
> and live in the hills,
> Among the sounds of music and the light
> Of waters, till the evil days are done.
> For here some terrible death is waiting you,
> Some unimagined evil, some great darkness
> That fable has not dreamt of, nor sun nor moon
> Scattered
>
> -----
>
> Let Him that made mankind, the angels and devils
> And dearth and plenty, mend what He has made,
> For when we labour in vain and eye still sees
> Heart breaks in vain.
>
> (pp. 25-26)

He offers her the world of her dreams. He mentions hills, music, light and water to tempt her away from the world of death, evil and darkness. She should take refuge in the world of dreams otherwise the world of duties would lead her towards a terrible region. The conflict between dreams and responsibilities was one of Yeats' own conflicts. Aleel tries to start the same conflict in Cathleen's mind. The diction that portrays the dream world stands in sharp contrast to the diction that draws the picture of the real world of misery. The juxtaposition of the two groups of images foregrounds the theme of good and evil. It also points out the futility of human efforts to put right the evil. Evil is not redeemable. Cathleen's sacrifice will be wasted. When Aleel fails to put his message across he resorts to the devil's tactics. He tries to deceive her by a subtle mixing of registers and saying that 'the old god' in his dreams that 'bid' (him) call (Cathleen) from these woods was 'angelical.' The epithet 'angelical' gives religious connotations to the signifier 'old God' that is secular. He attempts to create a confusion between secular and religious. But Cathleen's faith is not shaken. She knows that the old gods.

> Wander about the world to waken the heart
> The passionate, proud heart

Mixing of secular and sacred registers does not help the poet. Cathleen is too determined and discriminating to get confused. Notwithstanding the mixing of registers, persuasive tone and diplomatic style of speech, the illocutions of Allel fail to get the desired perlocutionary effect.

Cathleen can also discriminate between 'quiet' and 'peace.' She wants to heel a certain 'quiet' that torments her. And she yearns for 'peace.' The signifiers 'quiet' and 'peace' signify opposing states of mind. The idiolect of Cathleen attaches specific connotations to the two words. She knows the distinction between the two as well as she knew the distinction between 'the old god' and 'angelical.' She chooses her path with firm determination and absolute clarity of purpose. She is a heroic figure. Her language is an evidence to her stature. It is elevated.

> Cathleen : I have sworn
> By her whose heart the seven sorrows have pierced
> To pray before this altar until my heart
> Has grown to heaven like a tree, and there
> Rustled its leaves, till heaven has saved my people
> (p. 27)

Her faith in religion expresses itself in images from the world of nature as well as from the world of art -

> Cathleen : Old man, old man, He never closed a door
> Unless one opened. I am desolate
> Because of a strange thought that's in my heart;
> But I have still my faith; therefore be silent;
> For surely He does not forsake the world
> But stands before it modelling in the Clay

And molding there His image. Age by age
The clay wars with His fingers and pleads hard
For its old, heavy, dull and shapeless ease;
But sometimes - though His hand is on it still
It moves awry and demon hordes are born.

(p.33)

The image of God shaping man out of clay is very old. But Yeats, being Yeats, infused a new life into it. He made it his own. The clay is not just a passive agent moulded by God after his own will and image. It becomes an opponent, at war with Him. It resists being shaped. The variety of adjectives attached to the dull essence that man is made of draw a bright picture of it. The image is extended to include the source of demons. In substance man and demon are similar. But the demons are different from men as they have a higher ability to resist and affirm their own will. The secular mind betrays itself but only in some glimpses here and there. The later plays present the secular ideology in a positive light. The image keeps recurring during the play and becomes a unifying device. First it is used by Cathleen then it is used for her, with a significant extension.

So many pitchers of rough clay
Should prosper and the porcelain break in two.

(p. 46).

Yeats explores every possibility to create porcelain out of this clay modelling business. He carves a set of values upon them. Cathleen is the porcelain — the most precious soul. The simple villagers are 'pitchers of rough clay' — souls not wholly pure and refined.

The language of the unheroic peasant characters shows a marked difference from the language of Aleel and Cathleen — the heroic characters. Yeats records the rhythms of living speech in the dialogues of Mary and Teigue that open the play :

Mary : What can have made the grey hen flutter so ?

Teigue : They say that now the land is famine struck
The graves are walking

Mary : What can the hen have heard ?

Teigue : And that's not the worst; at Tuber-vanach
A woman met a man with ears spread out
And they moved up and down like a bat's wing.

Mary : What can have kept your father all this while !

(p. 3)

Teigue is excited with his own thoughts. He does not attend to the queries from his mother. He is self-engrossed. Mary's questions begin with a casual tone. As the tension builds up it shows itself in Mary's syntax. The paradigm of Mary's single sentence statement shows first a disappearance of an epithet and then a shift in the tone of her dialogue. The casual, informal tone changes to a tense and bitter one.

The images used by the peasant characters belong to the register of materialistic language. Shemus is a practical, down-to-earth fellow. He tells the demon merchants that in the evil days 'they rattle like knives in a basket.' When Oona-Cathleen's foster mother-finds Cathleen not responding to the requests from Aleel and herself she feels a sense of worthlessness. She feels that they are 'like flies upon a window pane.' The peasants pay simple yet poetic tributes to Cathleen -

'She was the great while lily of the world'
She was more beautiful than the pole star'
'The little plant I loved is broken in two'

(p.48)

Aleel's tributes are deeply emotional. His register of poetry is richer and fresher than the register of poetry used by the peasants. He feels as if he is reduced to a ball of passionate dust. Cathleen is transformed into a ball of dust. But Aleel has the burden of his passions that did not die with their object. The image reveals the intensity of his pathos. It is novel, intense and striking.

The peasant characters believe in 'human headed owls' and 'Men without eyes, ears and nose.' Gold, the gleaming yellow heaps of gold, capture their imagination. It wipes every thought of hell and damnation out of their minds. The concrete, the present fascinates them. The abstract, the future ceases to have meaning for them. The materialistic imagery emphasises the debasing materialism that determines their lives. They speak a stylized country dialect of Gaelic English. It is vividly expressive and suitable as a vehicle of immediate communication.

Shemus : When the hen's gone
What can we do but live on sorrel and dock
And dandelion, till our mouths are green ?

Mary : God, that to this hour has found bit and sup
Will cater for us still.

Shemus : His kitchen is bare
There were five doors that I looked through this day
And saw dead and not a soul to wake them.

(p.5)

'His kitchen is bare brings God down to the level of human world and robs him of grandeur. The casual tone, its lack of reverence and awe pull the all powerful down to the level of those who are helpless in the hands of some forces other than His. This attitude is developed in the later plays and relates to one of the basic tenets of Yeats' ideology and intention.

The language of the play shows a polarization towards heroic and peasant. On a different plane vocabulary themes are built up to depict the conflict between good and evil — the basic theme of the play. The vocabulary of the play shows the polarisation in two directions. — the forces of good and the forces of evil. The two are shown waging a perpetual battle. There are couples of images, the demon merchant is of 'the ninth and mightiest hell' whereas the Countess is 'the saint with sapphire eyes,' 'the heavenly host.' Heaven and hell, light and shadow, angels and devils pay the tug-of-war. They fight a pitched battle on the stage. The abstract is presented vividly, in a concrete form. The battle is presented dramatically, The heavenly grandeur is depicted in a narrative form.

The Angel : The light beats down; the gates of pearl are wide
And she is passing to the floor or peace
And mary of the seven times wounded heart
Has kissed her lips, and the long blessed hair
Has fallen on her face; the Light of Lights

Looks always on the motive not the deed
The shadow of shadows on the deed along

(p.50)

The vocabulary of the angels abounds in positive terms. Their tone is exalted. The language and tone of the demon merchants show a marked contrast in the concentration of words towards evil practices.

First Merchant : That may not be
We cannot face the heavenly host in arms
Her soul must come to us of its own will
But being of the ninth and mightiest Hell
Where all are kings, I have a plan to win her.

(p.29)

They have been making 'deals', 'bargaining' souls. Now they 'plan' to win her. The verbs show the activities belonging to the devil. Evil, according to the tenets of Christianity, is the absence or withdrawal or denial of good. Evil is negation. The language of evil is the language of negation.[1] Negation is present at different levels of language ranging from morphological and syntactical to the levels of semantics and interactive speech.

The demon merchants use techniques of negation at the interactive speech level. Their speech acts are directed towards persuading the peasants to do something that is not in their interest. They get a temporary success in getting their desired perlocutionary results. Their illocutions won them the souls of a few peasants. They also succeeded in making Cathleen sign for the sale of her soul which was their most ambitious goal. The success, though temporary, of the demon merchant's speech acts aroused violent hostility among the Irish audience. The Irish men and women took it to be a slur upon their honour that they could ever sell their souls to keep their bodies. The theatre managers had to stop the performance of *The Countess Cathleen* as a results of the crowd's violent response to it. The illocutions of the playwright were not received in their true spirit. Though after sometime the play regained its popularity.

THE LAND OF HEART'S DESIRE

In *The Countess Cathleen* the protagonist had chosen the path of sacrifice when the play began. Cathleen left little room for the success of speech acts performed by other characters to influence her decision. Mary — the heroine in *The Land of Heart's Desire* — leaves ample possibilities open for persuasion. She faces the conflict between her private dreams and her family responsibilities. The real drama consists of speech acts from her family members that want to guide her decision into the direction of duties and speech acts from the Faery Child who lures Mary to the land of her heart's desire. Mary Bruin stands at a point where she has to make a choice between the ordinary, material world and the supernatural existence. Instead of the opposition between peasant and heroic world views in *The Countless Cathleen* the action of *The Land of Heart's Desire* lies within folk tradition. Unlike Cathleen, who is a Christian being, Mary is an emotional, instinctive creature attracted and charmed by the pagan or faery land. As the representative of imagination and intuition Mary is at odds with her family and in harmony with the joyous and spontaneous life of fairy people.

Like the poet Aleel in *The Countess Cathlenn* Mary too eq uates the pagan and the Christian connotations of the register of spiritual language :

Mary : They have taken away the blessed quicken wood
They will not bring good luck into the house;
Yet I'm gland that I was courteous to them
For are they not, likewise, children of God ?

Father Hart : Coleen, they are the children of the fiend
And they have power until the end of time
When God shall fight with them a great
pitched battle
And hack them into pieces. (pp'. 57-8)

As the old God Aengus was angelical for Aleel, the Faery Child is the child of God for Mary. Her secular, pagan ideology is contrasted with the Christian ideology of Father Hart. Later on there are separate groups of images for the pagan and the Christian registers. The images of magical quicken wood, fire, milk are put in contrast to the images of crucifix, bread and wine. The light hearted ecstasy of the faery land is opposed to the monotonous existence of the life led by Father Hart. Mourteen, Bridget and Shawn :

Mary : Come, Faeries, take me out of this dull house!
Let me have all the freedom I have lost;
Work when I will and idle when I will!
Faeries, come take me out of this dull world
For I would ride with you upon the wind
Run on the top of the dishevelled tide,
And dance upon the mountains like a flame.

Father Hart : You cannot know the meaning of your words.

Mary : Father, I am right weary of four tongues
A tongue that is too crafty and too wise,
A tongue that is more bitter than the tide,
And a kind tongue too full of drowsy love
Of drowsy love and my captivity.

(p.61)

Mary's dialogues are marked by an intensity of lyricism that is rooted in her excessive sentimentality. Yeats came to think of the play as 'an exaggeration of sentiment and sentimental beauty'. He confessed in a latter to AE :

In my Land of Heart's Desire and in some of my lyric verse of that time, there is an exaggeration of sentiment and sentimental beauty which I have come to think unmanly. The popularity of 'The Land of Heart's desire' seems to me to come not from its merits but because of this weakness.... My own early subjectiveness rises at race moments and yours nearly always rises above sentiment to a union with a pure energy of the spirity....[2]

Yeats' intention was to elevate and to popularize poetic drama. This play was popular because of its non-elevation. Hence Yeats did not consider it a success. Yet, the sentimental lyricism of the play has its impact upon the listeners. Mary's paradigms of images of the fairy land and of the four tongues accelerate the tempo of the verse in the drama. Repetition of a syntagmatic pattern has its charm. The drama rises in intensity. It also denotes Mary's complete rejection of the material world.

The songs of the Fairy Child are even more intense in lyricism. When the child enters and repeats Mary's paradigm of four tongues, we are astonished. Even Mary is shocked and the realization that she is in the power of fairy people dawns upon her. Our initial feelings of shock are soon replaced by the understanding that the Fairy Child is in one sense the voice of Mary's own heart. This partially accounts for the success of the Fairy Child's speech acts. Repetition of a whole speech by a supernatural agency brings to the mind the action-suffering speech of Thomas Archbishop in Eliot's *Murder in the Cathedral*. Eliot made the Fourth Tempter — who represented Thomas's own deepest self-repeat his speech with which he entered the stage. Yeats makes the Fairy Child repeat Mary's speech describing the weariness of existence in this world. The repetition serves an important function. It tells us that Mary is an active protagonist and that the power of the Fairy Child upon her is only because of Mary's own willingness. She is indomitable. Only the illocutions that voice her own desire bring about successful perlocationary effect. The Fairy Child intensifies Mary's own desire with her allurements. She is a master at performing speech acts. Her illocutions never fail. She could make everyone dance to her tunes. Even Birdget granted her many favours giving milk, bread and honey. She coaxes Mary by calling her 'newly married bride,' 'little bird.' Finally, there is a king of tug-of-war of speech acts pulling Mary's choice in two opposing directions :

The Child : Stay and come with me, newly married bride,
For if you hear him you grow like the rest;
Bear children, cook, and bend above the churn
And wrangle over butter, fowl and eggs,
Until at last, grown old and bitter of tongue,
You're crouching there and shivering at the grave.

Father Hart : Daughter, I point you out the way to Heaven

The Child : But I can lead you, newly married bride
Where nobody gets old and crafty and wise,
Where nobody gets old and godly and grave,
Where nobody gets old and bitter of tongue,
And where kind tongues bring no captivity,
For we are but obedient to the thoughts
The drift into the mind at a wink of the eye.

Father Hart : It is because I put away the crucifix
That I am nothing, and my power is nothing
I'll bring it here again

Mounteen : No

Bridget : Dont leave us

Father Hart : O, let me go before it is too late;
It is my sin alone that brought it all.

The Child : I hear them sing, 'come, newly married bride,
Come to the woods and waters and pale lights.'

Mary : I will go with you

(p. 70)

Mary has been silent throughout the dialogue listening to both the sides. The child is more lively and appealing in her style of speech. She cancels out every argument put forward by Father Hart. Since Mary has already shown her inclination towards the dream world of faeries the speech acts of the child swiftly approach the heart of Mary. She shows a faint with to stay with Shawn but the attraction to the world of fulfilment of her dreams is irresistible. The persistence of the Fairy Child with her frequent luring dialogues compels Mary to go with her.

The language — patterned precise dialogues, emotional tone and luring style — of the Fairy Child finally wins her the 'newly married bride' for the fairy land. Her song 'the lonely of heart is withered away' and her dance are additional strengths. The lyricism of the song suggests an active supernatural presence. its repetition acts ad a structural device as it echoes words and phrases from Mary's speeches as well as from the dialogues of the Fairy Child herself. The play is integrated into a single whole largely by the device of repetition of the song and certain phrases and dialogues. The style of the play's language accounts for its beauty and popular appeal.

THE KING'S THRESHOLD

Conflict or struggle is the energy or vigour of life in Yeats' ideology. The conflict between dream and duty presented in the first plays is given a different turn.in this plays that enacts a conflict between action and words — the man of action and the man of letters are set in antagonism. The conflict is set off by an action on the King's part by which he takes back the ancient right of the poets to have a place in the King's Council. The King was pressurized by the nobles of his court. He is an objective man of responsibility in Yeats' system of beliefs. The poet is the subjective man of dreams. The King, like any other institution, cannot survive without chaining the anarchic freedom of individuals. It is also a conflict between individual freedom and social responsibility.

To reinstate the poet to its ancient place of honour, Seanchan — the chief poet of Ireland — sits on a fast. To persuade him break his fast there are different groups of tempters. These characters differ in their ideologies and their roles in society. Accordingly their illocutions differ in the choice of register and style of speech. They try to dissuade the poet from his chosen path that leads him to death. The poet has his own illocutions to resists the temptations from different quarters. The poet and his pupils speak a poetic, almost lyrical register of language.

The poet : I would have all know that when all falls
In ruin, poety calls out in joy,
Being the scattering hand, the bursting pod,
The victim's joy among the holy flame
God's laughter at the shattering of the world
And now that joy laughs out, and weeps and burns
On these bare steps

Youngest pupil : O, master, do not die !

(p.114)

After some arguments the pupils give up their efforts to persuade the Poet. Instead they go to the King to persuade him to restore the ancient right of the Poet. With his pupils the Poet's speech acts have succeeded. Though the King does not let them succeed. Nor would the Poet accept failure. Another direction of the Poet's success is his death. The pupils realize it and ask Seanchan, "Die, Seanchan and proclaim the right of the poets."

The King and the Chamberlain persuade the poet in a language that is formal in the tenor of discourse and rational and argumentative in the style of speech :

> Chamberlain : You wrong us, Seanchan
> There is none here but holds you in respect
> And if you'd only eat out of this dish
> The king would show how much he
> honours you.
>
> (p. 126)

He is very formal and rational in his approach. The King, though his office is more formal, is more informal and emotional in his tone than the Chamberlain. His pleading tenor and emotional approach show his relationship with the Poet. He is close in friendship to the Poet. But his arguments do not have much weight for Seanchan. There is a gap between his action and his words.

> The King : Seanchan, put away your pride as I
> Have put my pride away. I had your love
> Not a great while ago, and now you have planned
> To put a voice by every cottage fire,
> And in the night when no one sees who cries,
> To cry against me till my throne has crumbled,
> And yet if I give way I must offend
> My courtiers and nobles till they, too,
> Strike, at the crown. What would you have of me ?
>
> (p. 139)

The force of the king's illocutions fails to make a mark on the poet's determination. The poet is the hero — the indomitable individual who will not compromise his ideal.

Another quarters from which persuasions came are the monk and the soldier who represent two other institutions of State : church and law. For the monk discipline is the foremost value. He abhors the poet for his lack of discipline. He utterly lacks any sympathy for the poet.

> Monk : Certainly, I will not
> I've made too many homilies, wherein
> The wanton imagination of the poets

Has been condemned, to be his flatterer
If pride and disobedience are unpanished
Who will obey ?

(p. 123)

The poet does not recognize the authority of church. That is why the monk is so harsh. He completely fails to see and virtue in the poet's ideal. His words wanton, condemn, flatter, pride, disobedience, unpunished display his arrogance and bitterness. He is not competent to perform speech-acts. The soldier is the bitterest in tone. He denotes physical force. The power of words is not recognized by him.

Soldier : I will not interfere, and if he starve
For being obstinate and stiff in the neck
'tis but good riddance.

(p. 124)

He shows an utter lack of understanding of the poet's motive. His speech is very sharp and brief. He cannot see any reason in a man's sacrifice of life for an ideal that is very trivial for him. He too is utterly incompetent at performing speech acts. Their speeches defeat their purpose.

It contrast to the speeches of the monk and the soldier. We have the humourous speeches of Brian that are in rich provincial dialect. The dialect carries a greater illocutionary force with it.

Brain : Master, eat this, it is not king's food that is cooked for every body and nobody. Here's barley-bread out of your father's oven and dulse from Duras. Here's the dulse. Your honour, it is wholesome, it has the good taste of the sea.

(p.117)

The register of comic prose used by Brian brings great relaxation to the audience's minds which have been over-taxed by the quarrelsome, argumentative styles of other characters' speeches. The Mayor and the Cripples too use the register of prose and a comic style. The Mayor's speeches are as absurd as his behavior. Whereas the cripples, though imperfect in the body, show a greater soundness of spirit and mind. They are the most sympathetic characters to the cause of the poet. They share their view of poetry with the poet. But being the common, unheroic people their language is very simple.

Their simple prose register stands out in contrast to the elevated poetic register of the poet and his pupils. Their style of language emphasizes the lonely pride of the heroic character.

First cripple : It would serve the King right if seanchan drove away his luck. What's there is a king that's in the world from birth to burial like another man, that he should change old customs that were in it as long as the world has been a world?

Second cripple : If I were the King, I wouldn't meddle with him, there is a something queer about a man that makes rhymes....

Their prose is, however, not prosaic. It is close to poetry in its idiom and rhythm. it is loose in syntax and simple in diction but powerful in rhythm and elevated in ideas. They are openly selfish as contrasted with the hypocrisy of other characters like the monk, the soldier and Chamberlain. Their values are contrasted with the values represented by the court ladies. The court ladies are the innocent agents of corruption as Seanchan's image of lepers reveals. Their persuasions too do not succeed. Even the persuasions of Fedelm — the most forceful ones — fail to achieve the desired goal.

The failure of the Speech acts of different characters, like in the other plays, foregrounds the victory of the heroic figure. Yeats' ideal of hero is a proud, indomitable creature. The poet succeeds in his goal as the pupils recognise :

Not what it leaves behind it in the light
But what it carries with it to the dark
Exalts the soul.

(p.143)

Seanchan's death is surrounded by romantic heroics. These oft-quoted lines are an eloquent speech act from the playwright to sing success of the poet. The play is a direct eloquent speech in favour of Yeats' proclaimed goal — revival of poetry in the theatre.

THE SHADOWY WATERS

The plays demonstrates Yeats' further experiments with the mixing of the registers of prose and poetry in order to elevate and popularize drama. He revised the play with the aim to strengthen its poetry with common language and to get what he called 'creaking shoes' and 'liquorice-root' into abstract speech. He combined poetry with common passion by a closer approximation to the rhythms of colloquial speech. The high art and low style are put together to set of each other. The revised version uses prose for minor characters. It has a sharper delineation of individual characters. It has its symbolism reduced. Still they play remains highly symbolic and a considerable distance exists between the surface level and its symbolic significance. Yeats takes celtic myth and loads it with his private system of philosophy. The language bears the burden of different layers of symbolic meaning. The play is raised to the level of a ritual in its rhythm, styles of speech and movements of the actors. Though the surface register of language is very simple and common.

The sailors speak a peasant dialect that is in the register of prose. But on the deeper level it is poetic in its images, phrases and syntax :

> First sailor : I will strike him first. No! For that music of his might put a beast's head upon my shoulder, or it may be two heads and they devouring one another.

The prose is rich in imagination and informal in style. Yeats makes abrupt changes from verse to prose and prose to verse. The jolt in moving from one to the other reinforces the implication of the play. When he passes from prose to verse in this play, raising the tone of the language, he gives a strong impression of the inadequacy of the human world. At one place in the play the dichotomy between the real and the dream worlds is strongly underlined by the strategy of prose-and-verse : when Aibric and the sailors move away from Forgael and his birds, prose-reality and poetry-reality equally claim a place on the stage, though Forgael alone captures the audience attention :

> Second Sailor : There is nobody is natural but a robber. That is the reason the whole world goes tottering about upon its bandy legs.

Aibric : Run upon the, now, and overpower the crew while yet asleep.

As Aibric and the sailors go out Forgael, who remains at the tiller, cries out :

There ! There ! They come ! Gull, gannet, or diver,
But with a man's head, or a fair woman's.
They hover over the masthead awhile
To wait their friends, but when their friends have come
They'll fly upon that secret way of theirs,
One - and one - cauple - five together ... (0.153)

The prose-to-verse device sets off the full significance of poetry which is the appropriate language for the dream reality that exists in the imagination of Forgael. Yeats also experiments with the transformation of prose into poetry, in this play. It illuminates the intensity of the protagonist's feeling and its impact on other characters. The colloquial register of the sailors speeches is replaced by a lyrical register after the transformation of Dectora's passion which sends lyrical waves in all the directions. The speeches of the sailors are elevated in rhythm.

First Sailor : I saw a sken of ale aboard her - a pigskin of brown ale

Third Sailor : Come to the ale, a pig skin of brown ale, a goatskin of yellow !

First Sailor : Brown ale and yellow; yellow and brown ale; a goatskin of yellow !

All : Brown ale and yellow; yellow and brown ale!

(p. 159)

The repetitions produce an effect of ritual. The mysterious transformation of Dectora's feelings that has been effected by Forgael's playing upon the magical harp casts its spell upon other characters. The turning point is further emphasized by the elevation of the Sailor's loose prose to song.

The more formal tenor and richer ornamentation of the heroic speeches are strengthened by the use of images from the register of common language. The more heroic character Aibric's speeches are closer in texture to colloquial speech.

Aibric : The hold is full - boxes of precious spice,
Ivory images with amethyst eyes,
Dragons with eyes of ruby. The whole ship
Flashes as if it were a net of herrings
Let us return to our own country, Forgael,
And spend it there. Have you not found this queen ?
What more have you to look for on the seas ?

(p.165)

Forgael — the protagonist — speaks a different register of language. He is governed by some passion that is not of this world. His speeches are full of 'wild words.' He seems to be 'muttering' in dream. he speaks of some 'pale forehead' and 'hair that is the colour of burning' — his dream image. He could hear birds passing which the sailors did not notice. The birds are his pilots. Every thing about him is surrounded in mystery. The birds are to lead him to some 'unheard of passion' that the world knows nothing about. He cannot 'argue' about his dreams. The supernatural realities are beyond reason or intellect. He expresses his inability to communicate with others and convince them —

Forgael : I cannot answer
I can see nothing plain; all is mystery
Yet sometimes there's a torch inside my head.
That makes all clear, but when the light is gone
I have but images, analogies,
The mystic bread, the sacramental wine,
The red rose where the two shafts of the cross,
Body and soul, waking and sleep, death, life,
Whatever meaning ancient allegorists
Have settled on, are mixed into one joy
For what's the rose than that ? Miraculous cries
Old stories about mystic marriages
Impossible truths ? But when the torch is lit
All that is impossible is certain
I plunge in the abyss.

(p.152)

Forgael struggles with the register of poetry to communicate his spiritual vision of ideal union and reconciliation of opposites in nature. The mystic vision that the poet sees in a moment of revelation defies definition. In his efforts to convey the real nature of that moment of tragic joy when 'the torch is lit' Forgael accumulates images for the registers ot philosophy, mysticism, religion and poetry. The mind fails to grasp the miracle in a precise way. Different symbols and analogies float into his mind. The moment when what seems impossible to the intellect is made certain is the moment of mystical marriage of contraries. That in Yeats' system of beliefs is the moment of individual's fulfilment and achievement of the unity of being. As the moment moves nearer actualization Forgael's speeches becomes highly pitched — charged with passion and excitement.

Forgael : There are some
That weigh and measure all in these waste seas
They that have all the wisdom that's in life,
And all that prophesying images
Made of dim gold rave out in secret tombs :
They have it that the plans of kings and queens
Are dust on the moth's wing; that nothing matters
But laughter and tears - laughter, laughter and tears -
That everyman should carry his own soul
Upon his shoulders.

(p. 155)

Yeats' ideal always consists of a pair of opposites — opposites hammered into unity — for example 'laughter and tears.' There is always a struggle between sets of opposing forces in this universe that strive towards unification. It is one of Yeats' basic ideological tenets.

Yeats believed in the capacity of tragic art to attain that ideal unity. "Tragic art, passionate art, the drowner of dykes, the confounder of understanding, moves us to reverie by alluring us almost to the intensity of trance. The persons upon the stage, let us say, greaten till they are humanity itself. We feel our minds expand convulsively or spread out slowly like some moon-brightened, image crowded sea. That which is before our eyes perpetually vanishes and returns again in the midst of the excitement it creates, and the more enthralling it is, the more do we forget it."[2] The music of Forgael's harp works as a drowner of dykes, The differences of individual characters are melted. They resonate each other's ideas. There is a oneness of rhythm and tone on the stage. All speak the same register of dream language.

Aibrie : .. O! O! O! O! O! O!
For golden armed Iollan has been killed.

Dectora : ... And that he died a thousand years ago.
O! O! O! O! O!

(p. 160-61)

The repetition of wailing exclamations further submerges the dykes and intensifies the tragic experience. All are set to reverie — made to travel into the dark interior of the mind. They do not see what is but see the vision that the music leads them to. The present becomes obliterated into a distant past. The music of the magic harp changes the human figures into superhuman creatures. The differences of human and superhuman too are merged. The speeches of Forgael, and his harp music, has achieved this wonderful feat. The essential unity of the inner drama is brought to the foreground.

Forgael has remained, during most of the play, possessed by a strange, mysterious passion that is superhuman is intensity. He listens to the messages in birds' cries and follows them. Dectora too, charmed by the harp music, chooses to go with Forgael. The final speeches from the entranced couple are highly elevated in language and intensely rhythmic in lyricism. The moment of fulfilment requires highly poetic expression. The moment that is most dramatic is rendered in the most poetic language :

Dectora : Bend lower, O king, that I may crown you with it.
O flower of the branch, O bird among the leaves,
O silver fish that my two hands have taken
Out of the running stream, O morning star,
Trembling in the blue heavens like a white fawn
Upon the misty border of the wood,
Bend lower, that i may cover you with my hair,
For we will gaze upon this world no longer,
(the harp begins to burn as with fire)

Forgael : (Gathering Dectora's hair about him)
Beloved, having dragged the net about us,
And knitted mesh to mesh, we grow immortal;
And that old harp awakens of itself
To cry aloud to the grey birds, and dreams,
That have had dreams for father, live in us

(p. 167)

Piling up of metaphors in Dectora's speech is an evidence that Yeats was making his audience conscious of the presence of poetry. He intended to re-establish poetry in the theatre. The audience were supposed to appreciate poety being aware that it was poetry. But Yeats came to think of the poetry in this play as faulty. In a letter to Arthur & Symons of 10 September 1905 Yeats analysed the weakness of *The Shadowy Waters :*

> One thing I am now quite sure of is that all the finest, poetry comes logically out of the fundamental action, and that the error of late periods like this is to believe that some things are inherently poetical, and to try and pull them on to the scene at every moment, it is just these seemingly inherently poetical things that wear out. My *Shadowy Waters* was full of them, and the fundamental thinking was nothing, and that gave the whole poem an impression of weakness. There was no internal life pressing for expression through the characters.[3]

Yeats was a constant reformer. Though this play was outlined by Yeats when he was till at school its first publication took place in 1900. Not satisfied with its performance he revised it thoroughly after 1905. The 1907 version was drastically different in characterisation and symbolism from its earlier version. And Dectora's advertisingly poetic speech to Forgael "has an animation and a poetic logic which is very far from Donogue's description of it as "tossing mere wool-balls of Pre-Raphaelite lyricism."[4]

DEIRDRE

Deirdre like Dectora in *The Shadowy Waters* Chooses a heroic though tragic path embodying Yeats' paradigm of tragic joy. But in *Deirdre* the distance between the surface level of episodes and characters and their symbolic or philosophic significance has been squeezed further as compared to *The Shadowy Waters*. The scheme of conflict is pursued though the area of conflict is shifted. Conchubar and Naoise represent the universal conflict of old age and youth, honour and passion, public and private morality. The play takes place entirely on a human plane, showing human passions and psychology.

The language remains consistently poetic. The register of poetry does not show any sharp fluctuations for the most part. It is unified throughout. It has no polarisations like heroic and peasant registers. The blank verse rhythm is maintained for all the characters except for the lyrics of the musicians that Yeats introduced in this play. The regularity of blank verse is broken once more in the scene between Conchubar and Deirdre, Deirdre's passing runs high while she pleads for Naoise's life. She used shortened sense units and parenthetical expressions. Here tone becomes frenzied :

Deirdre : It was my fault. I only should be punished
The very moment these eyes fell on him
How could he refuse ? At first he would not -
I'm not lying - he remembered you
What do I say ? My hands ? No no my lips -
For I had pressed my lips upon his lips -
I swear it is not false - my breast to his;
Until I woke the passion that's in all,
And how could he resist ? I had my beauty.
(p.197)

The musicians are Yeats' addition to the original legend. They act as a chorus, supplying exposition and background information for the action as well as objective commentary on the events and intimations of its outcome. They complement and extend Deirdre's persons. They are given simple poetic speeches like other characters. They also sing songs punctuating the play at certain significant moments. Their speeches are arcane in style. They do not speak out facts plainly. They hint at real facts. Their cryptic comments reveals the truth to the audience and the protagonist, establishing a direct link between the characters on the stage and audiences across the stage :

First Musician : I have heard he love you
As some old miser loves the dragon stone
He rides among the cobwebs near the roof.

Deirdre : You mean that when a man who has loved
like that
Is after crossed, love drowns in its own flood,
And that love drowned and floating is but hate;
And that a king who hates sleeps ill at night

Till he has killed; and that, thought the
day laughs,
We shall be dead at cock-crow

First Musician : You've not my thought
When I lost one I loved distractedly,
I blamed my crafty rival and not him,
And fancied, till my passion had run out,
That could I carry him away with me,
And tell him all my love, I'd keep him yet.

Deirdre : Ah ! now I catch your meaning, that this king
Will murder Naoise, and keep me alive

First Musician : 'tis you that put that meaning upon words
Spoken at random.

Deirdre : Wanderers like you
Who have their wits alone to keep their lives,
Speak nothing that is bitter to the ear
At random; if they hint at it at all
Their eyes and ears have gathered it so lately
That it is crying out in them for speech.

(p.182)

Their random manner of speech is the most precise and sharp. Deirdre picks up their meaning remarkably fast. Their indirect revelations voice Deirdre's own fears. Their style of speech creates an immediate communication link between the listeners on the stage and audiences across the stage. They put the audiences into the Supreme possession of knowledge. They are a source of immense knowledge. They know about the preparations for a wedding feast at Conchubar's palace and decorations of a bridal chamber there. They know the real intentions of Conchubar and they strengthen and support Deirdre's designed sacrifice in case of being forced to become Conchubar's queen.

The songs of the wandering musicians intensify the drama and elevate the play's language on the poetic scale. They demonstrate Yeats' control of lyric construction and integration. The songs reinforce and integrate the ideas in the play. Their exalted rhythms elevate the play.

The image of the chessboard, the dark faced soldiers, capture of Naoise like a bird integrate the verbal modes of discourse with visual modes. The register of game is a register of heroic battle as well — the battle for Deirdre. The chessboard is present on the stage. The surface register of the game connotes the deeper level of heroic combat. The deeper significance is further exploited through the frequent reappearance of dark faced soldiers on the stage. These black pawns support Conchubar and capture Naoise and eliminate him from the game — quite ignominously. After Naoise's death Deirdre recovers her heroic stature that had given way to her human anxieties for Naoise's safety in her scene with Conchubar. Her language returns to the natural rhythms of blank verse that mark her calm determination and a full control of the situation. He calm, followed by her frenzy, stands out in a marked contrast. The surface calm is only a device to deceive the king. It conceals a wild heart underneath. Yeats' protagonists are nothing if not wild when forced to act against their natural selves. The mask of quiet helps Deirdre outmaneuvre Conchubar in his designs. Her final speech is spoken in such a style and tone that it communicates dual meanings : one for the king, another for the musicians and the audience. So skillfully does she speak that the King fails to suspect the real significance of her words.

Deirdre : Now strike the wire, and sing to it s while
Knowing that all is happy, and that you know
Within what bride-bed, I shall lie this night
And by what man, and lie close up to him,
For the bed's narrow and there outsleep the cock crow
(p. 201)

Deirdre who failed in her speech acts with the king succeeds in her speech acts with the musicians and the audience.

THE GREEN HELMET

The language of *The Green Helment* marks a development in Yeats' efforts to fashion a verse form that suits his drama. He makes use of a line of fourteen syllables. He manages to overcome the tyranny of black verse as the only form of verse for drama. The fourteener is a heroic line — the pre-Renaissance form of metre that allows Yeats a greater freedom to capture a wider range of feelings. It is appropriate for the light jest of the Red man as well as for the heroic wrath of Cuchulain.

> Cuchulain - Old herring - you whip off heads ! why, then
> Whip off your own, for it seems you can clap it on again
> Or else go down in the sea, go down in the sea, I say
> Find that old juggler Mananan and whip his head away.
>
> (p. 231)

Cuchulain is heroic and shows his defiance in the beginning of the play where his speeches are marked by a tone of determination. He dismisses the attempts of Legaire and Conall to send him away from the place. His heroic defiance before Conall and Legaire and wrath before the Red Man show a dramatic change as a result of the Red Man's jestful attitude. he changes into a person of calm judgement and wisdom. They rhythm and style of his dialogues show a change accordingly.

> Cuchulain : I did not take it to keep it - The Red Man gave it for one,
> But I shall give it to all - to all of us three or to none;
> That is an you look upon it - we will pass it to and fro
> And time and time about, drink out of it and so
> Stroke into peace this cat that has come to take our lives.
>
> (p. 233).

The slow rhythms, long sentences denote a wisdom that resolves various conflicts presented in the play : the quarrel to decide the person who deserves the Helmet best; the quarrel of the wives of three brothers as to who will enter the gate first; the conflict regarding the Red man's claim to whip off the head of one of the brothers. Cuchulain's efforts to resolve these conflicts are thwarted by the Red man - his anti-self. But ultimately the Red Man is won over by Cuchulain's heroic magnanimity and rewards him with the offer of the Helmet.

Once again Yeats integrates the visual mode of presentation with the verbal mode. He experiments with colour imagery to present the antagonisms. The colour scheme distances the action from everyday reality and elevates it to the superhuman levels. The setting is directed to be orang-red and black with tinges of purple. The characters of the heroic nature are dressed in various shades of green - the green of helmet. Through the open doors and windows green is repeated in the shining of the sea. The supernatural figure antagonistic to Cuchulain is the Red man dressed in red. The importance of the colour scheme is pronounced and strong. Meaningful relationships are underlined by skillful colour scheme. Red and green are complementary in one sense and contradictory in another. Red and green were meaningful symbols in Christianity as well as in early fertility cults. These varying fields of association link modern Ireland with the Celtic past. The same signifiers 'red' and 'green' signify different things in different contexts - contexts of religion, mythology and art.

The songs mark a deviation from the basic mood and rhythms of the play. The songs are written in very short and emphatic lines. The boastful song 'Laegaire is best' is in regular and heavily accented diametres. Emer's song 'Nothing that he has done' is modulated by occasional trimetres which add to its emotional force. Songs mark a higher elevation of language on the scale of poetry. They are sung at dramatically significant moments to heighten the intensity of action and communicate its real meaning and significance.

ON BAILE'S STRAND

Yeats intended this play for popular audience. The action is presented on a realistic plane. The action, however, has a layered pattern. The central episode is Cuchulain's oath and its consequences. The Cuchulain who would tame the hawk woman and prove himself worthy of the hero's crown in seen facing a dilemma and making a tragic choice that reflects his fall from the unity of being. The pressures of social responsibility tame Cuchulain's wild anarchic self. On the heroic plane Cuchulain is presented in opposition to Conchubar. Cuchulain represents action and intuition. Conchubar is a man of reason and moderation. This is the central layer of action. On a different level another sequence of action involving a blind man and a fool echoes and reinforces whatever meaning the heroic figures represent. The action presented on two parallel planes — heroic and mundane — enriches the drama.

The characters on the heroic plane speak in an elevated register of language : a poetic field of discourse, and a formal tenor of discourse. Conchubar is a man of practical insight and rational outlook. His speeches are marked by high formality and a placidity of tone. He argues and persuades Cuchulain to take the oath of obedience. Though not a man of action like Cuchulain he performs successful speech acts. His illocutions to subdue Cuchulain's anarchic freedom are rewarded with Cuchulain's taking the oath. Cuchulain on the other hand is the man of action who carries out the real action in the drama — he takes the oath, fights the battle in which he unknowingly kills his own son, and finally leaves the stage to fight the surging sea.

Cuchulain's language shows high fluctuations during the course of drama. Being a man of intuition and impulse his moods change very frequently and suddenly. While he argues with the High King about taking the oath his speech is argumentative and tone balanced. But at the mention of children it shows a rise in temper. As soon as the emotional chord is touched he is excited. The rhythms of his dialogue and carried to a high pitch when Aoife — his wild love — is mentioned. He speaks as if in a dream.

Cuchulain : Ah ! Conchubar, had you seen her
With that high, laughing turbulent lead of hers
Thrown backward, and the bow string at her ear
Or sitting at the fire with those grave eyes
Full of good counsel as it were with wine
Or when love run through all the lineaments
Of her wild body - although she had no child
None other had all beauty, queen or lover,
Or was so fitted to give birth to kings.

(pp. 258-9)

He is quite eloguent while enumerating memories of Aoife. The rhythm picks up a momentum. It abounds in images.

Cuchulain : No wonder in that, no wonder at all in that
I never have known love but as a kiss

In the mid-battle, and a difficult truce
Of oil and water, candles and dark night
Hillside and hollow, the hot footed sun
And the cold, sliding, slippery-footed moon -
A brief forgiveness between opposites
That have been hatreds for three times the age
Of this long-established ground.

(p. 259)

As the emotion builds up, the tempo rises and language takes on lyrical overtones. The wildest possible definition of love is given by Cuchulain - Yeats' most ferocious young hero of Irish legends.

When the same Cuchulain is chained by the oath of obedience to the king the wildness drowns into wisdom. His speeches, then become low pitched and are without fluctuations. As the spirits tone down the rhythms slow down.

Cuchulain : I understand it all
It's you that have changed. You've wives and
children now
And for that reason cannot follow one
That lives like a bird's flight from tree to tree
It's time years put water in my blood
And drowned the wildness of it, for all's changed
But that unchanged - I'll take what oath you will
The moon, the sun, the water, light, or air,
I donot care how binding.

(p.261)

Cuchulain's register of language, style of speech and tone of dialogue are changed. Words like 'understand' and 'reason' enter his vocabulary. The emotional force has been withdrawn and replaced by an intellectual tone, foregrounding the hero's fall from his unity of being. He becomes cool and 'biddable.' But the final line 'I do not care how binding' betrays Cuchulain's wildness even in his surrender. It seems that only the direction is changed. His passionate ferocity does not completely drown. He will either be free like a bird or will surrender entirely to the oath. The discipline of arbitrary wisdom prevails only for a short while. When the young man from Aife's country comes to the court of Conchubar and challenges Cuchulain to war all restraint is gone with the wind.

Cuchulain : The High King there has promised me his wisdom;
But the Hawk's sleepy till its well beloved
Cries out amid the acorns, or it has seen
Its enemy like a speck upon the sun
What's wisdom to the hawk, when that clear eye
Is burning nearer up in the high air ?

(p. 265)

He feels an intuitive friendliness for the young man. Cuchulain faces a dilemma between wisdom and intuition. The clear eye of intuition defies wisdom. The hawk in him denies any suppression from reason. The rhetorical self-interrogation presents the heroic fire that burns in him. But unfortunately the heroic tradition goes to a fall. Wisdom is made to prevail over heroic impulse. It leads to the final catastrophe where Cuchulain kills his own son. By showing Cuchulain's dilemma through splitting his speeches into the language and tone of intuition and the language and tone of reason that lead him to the disaster which needs no words but a desperate action on Cuchulain's part who goes to fight the mighty sea Yeats manipulates audience response and directs it successfully in the direction he desires. The audience feel wrath at the injustice meted out to the protagonist because he was not allowed to be his natural self. Yeats believed in the validity of intuition that has deeper roots in the mind of an individual and keeps in contract with the collective consciousness. He provides evidence in favour of his ideology.

The language of the blind man and the fool is colloquial as opposed to the poetry of Conchubar and Cuchulain. They speak is a different register — the register of prose. Their tenor of discourse too is different — it is informal. The contrast between the anti-heroic, mundane world of the blind man and the fool and the heroic ideal world of Cuchulain and Conchubar is reinforced and foregrounded by their language. Yeats has scrupulously maintained a balance and integration between colloquial prose and elevated poetry.

The speeches of the blind man and the fool are divided into short phrases and sentences giving them the rhythms of random speech and a colloquial quality. The shortened sense units and varied rhythms make their speeches light and gay -

The Blind Man : You have no wits to understand such things. He will sit up in this chair and he'll say : 'Take the oath, Cuchulain, I bid you take the oath. Do as I tell you what are your wits compared with mine and what are your riches compared with mine ? And what sons have you to pay your debts and to put a stone over you when you die? Take the oath, I tell you, take a stony oath.

Fool : I will not. I'll take no oath I want my dinner.

Blind Man : Hush, Hush ! It is not done yet.

Fool : You said it was done to a turn.

Blind Man : Did I, now ? The wings might be white but the legs might be red. The flesh might stick hard to the bones and not come away in the teeth. But, believe me, fool, it will be well done before you put your teeth in it.

Fool : My teeth are grown long with hunger.

(pp. 249-50)

The blind man is very shrewd and witty. To keep the fool's mind involved with the tale he tells it in a manner that keep his curiosity alive. His tactful revelations. bit by bit, succeed to keep the fool's thoughts away from dinner. The fool is performing speech acts. He is a man of words, like Conchubar, and his illocutions derive intended prelocutions. His attitude to the story and fate of Cuchulain is that of detachment. His light manner robs the solemnity off the real event when it takes place.

The blind man provides us with a version of Conchubar's speech to Cuchulain. It is interesting and significant to note the differences between his version and the actual speech. The discrepancy foregrounds Yeats' conscious efforts to make his audiences aware of the element of artifice in the style of his language.

Conchubar : Most certainly
I am high kind, my son shall be high king.
And you for all the wildness of your blood
And though your father came out of the sun
Are but a little king and weight but light

In anything that touches government -
If put into the balance with my children.
(p. 256)

The speech of Conchubar is not as direct and simple as the speech of the blind man. Besides, it is in the register of poety whereas the blind man spoke in colloquial prose. The mixing of the registers of prose and poetry in the play's language serves important functions. The prose of the fool and the blind man represents the life of unheroic circumstances in contrast to Cuchulain's heroism. But the prose is not simply a device to present antagonistic planes of existence, it is essential for the play. The fool and the blind man are much more significant in the spectacle they present on the stage than in the language they speak. The language has to take a subordinate place if the visual import is to be stressed. Poetry cannot subordinate itself in the manner that prose can.

Yeats, by á judicious use of various features of language, succeeds to present the drama with full force and gain popular appeal. *On Baile's Strand* is described by Parkinson as 'among the best poetic plays of the century' and as resolving 'almost perfectly what Yeats saw as the dramatist's general problem.' it deserves the tribute because of its "fully unified complexity, the archetypal power of its theme and the manner in which language and situation are made responsible to an almost Sophoclean power of structural irony."[12]

FOUR PLAYS FOR DANCERS

The dance plays are a significant milestone in Yeats' career as a verse playwright. The publication of *Four Plays for Dancers* marked an extension of Yeats' scheme of conflict to the level of literary genre. Yeats sought to hammer the two genres of lyric poetry and drama into a unified whole in his dance plays. "I need a theatre : I believe myself to be a dramatist"; "I have always felt that my work is not drama but the ritual of a lost faith."[5] This is the crux of conflict that exists in Yeats' dramatic theory and in his plays. He was always moving away from dramatic realism yet never diminished dramatic intensity. Dramatic action was unified with its anti-self lyrical intensity. Both the dramatic and the lyrical are taken to a higher level of elevation to emphasize the element of ritual that Yeats strove to rediscover in his dance plays. He distanced his drama in order to write "remote, spiritual, and ideal"[6] drama to move towards the archetype, he exalted the level at which the drama was performed. The drama is performed at a remote, mythical level. Drama gives direct expression to reverie. It is the speech of the soul with itself. The ritual, the remote, the mythical and the dream elements demand extreme intensity and stylization of language. A high degree of tension is generated into the language of drama. Language has to give direct expression to what defies expression most in the form of words. The register of language that suits such a purpose is the incantatory language. Songs and dance are necessary elements that elevate the play's language to remote heights.

Knowing that his ideal form of drama will not fulfil the demands of commercialism Yeats decided to be satisfied with a small audience — a drawing room audience. He set out to attain elevation at the expense of popularization, widening of the elevation gyre that implied a contraction of popularity gyre. His choice leads him into a direction that good opposite to the path chosen by Eliot. Eliot, in the middle of his career, decided to make his language transparent by putting 'poetry on a thin diet.' He sought to win a larger audience at the expense of dramatic and linguistic elevation. Yeats opted to pursue elevation and gave it a big push with his dance plays. The dance plays mark a break away from naturalism in every aspect of drama and a move towards stylization which allows a focus upon words and an emphasis upon the element of ritual :

> The theatre of art, when it comes to exist, must therefore discover grave and decorative gestures ... and grave and decorative scenery that will be forgotten the moment an actor has said, 'It is dawn' and dresses of so little irrelevant magnificence that the mortal actors and actresses may change without much labour into the immortal people of romance. The theatre began in ritual, and it cannot come to its greatness again without recalling words to their ancient sovereignity.[7]

The challenge before Yeats was to discover an appropriate language and to transform ideas into action — action that is dramatic as well as stylized. Yeats faces the challenge in his dance plays : *At the Hawk's Well, The Only Jealousy of Ember, The Dreaming of the Bones, Calvary.*

The dance plays that mark the climax on the scale of poetic elevation demonstrate a clear stamp of classical Noh drama of Japan. Music, dance, mask, myths and the method of symbolic representation in Noh drama provided a model for Yeats' plays. Yeats moulded the model according to his individual needs and ideal. The austere stylization answered Yeats' search for ritual in drama. In Yeats as well as in Noh poetry emerges through symbols and ideas : The dance plays "take us into a king of no-place inhabited by figures who are more often than not, anonymous — old man, young man, Queen, king — archetypal beings free of period and nationality."[9] Their poetry truly exists when elevated into the dimension of a static art at its climatic point. This is the moment of highest intensity that is reached by a combination of the elements of poetry, dance and rhythm. Dance occurs at the climatic moment and dissolves the tension making a transcendent calm prevail in the theatre. A lofty emotional frenzy followed by a moment of sublime scrutiny is the essential characteristic feature of Noh drama.

Universal or archetypal patterns are created out of what seems to be the topical or local : Ideas that have been "conceived not in the brain but in the whole body," wrote Yeats in his 'Certain Noble Plays of Japan.' Economy or austerity in every aspect of the play is the governing principle in the Noh as well as in Yeats' Noh inspired drama. They are very sparing of words and movement. Their ideal of beauty is cold, detached, remote and unresponsive to sensuousness. Their ideal of music is the music of 'silence,' of tension, of discontinuity or pause. Though the silence has a positive meaning and enables one to feel immense depth and a sense of infinity. Their ideal of movement is 'stillness' in their characters.

The express the depth of experience Yeats emphasized rhythm and movement :

> ... the purpose of rhythm, it has always seemed to me, is to prolong the moment of contemplation, the moment when we are both asleep and awake, which is the one moment of creation, by hushing as with an alluring monotony, while it holds us waking by variety, to keep us in that state of

> perhaps real trance, in which the mind liberated from the pressure of the will is unfolded in symbols.[8]

The trance moment embodies the real poetry of the Noh. The particular is elevated to the level of universal with the help of a number of dramatic and linguistic features. The characters wear masks that make them remote, strange and representative of some archetypal being. Yeats had expressed his wish to have masks which were 'images of those profound emotions that exist only in solitude and in silence'. The principle of 'controlled spontaneity' governs the use of mask in Noh. "Their mask is more subtly, imaginatively and suggestively dramatic than any actor's face can ever be."[10] The emphasis in Noh drama, as in Yeats' plays in on the revelatory, instead of concealing, function of mask. Rhythm, dance, mask and movement are the kinds of stylized aids to the words of which this drama is so sparing : these are various features of expression — the function of language.

AT THE HAWK'S WELL

Music, dance, mask, movement, in addition to speech, prepare the audience to receive the full impact of the drama in *At the Hawk's Well.* "The elements cohere; their coherence is the poetry of the play."[11] The strength of the play lies in its structure that is knit into a coherent, rhythmic pattern.

The dramatic conflict at the centre of the play, *At the Hawk's Well,* is enacted by multiplying relationships. The relationships are woven into a coherent pattern. Cachulain — the objective hero, confronts the women of Sidhe — the subjective counterpart. As an active and instinctive young man he is set in opposition to the passive and wise old man. In the one hand the antagonism is between the supernatural and natural, on the other the heroic and unheroic are put in opposition. The old man shares the qualities of the desolate scene that he inhabits. The register of language that describes the scene also describes the old man :

> First Musician : He is all doubled up with age
> The old thorn trees are doubled so
> Among the rocks where he is climbing (p. 201)

He is hard to be distinguished from the scene :

Cuchulain : You should be native here, for that rough
tongue
Matches the barbarous spot.

(p. 212)

He represents Cuchulain's opposite mode of conduct. He is afraid of Cuchulain's insolent youth and heroism. He fears that Cuchulain will not let him drink the water from the well. He tries to persuade Cuchulain to leave the place. But his illocutions are, like him, lifeless and fail to make any impact upon Cuchulain's determination. The passivity of age has to give way to the dynamism of youth.

The speeches of the old man and the young man are similar in their tenor of discourse and style of verse-register. Both use a formal tenor and iambic pentametre form of verse. The verse form is sometimes varied to give it naturalness.

Old Man : I came like you
When young in body and in mind, and blown
By what had seemed to me a lucky sail.
The well was dry, I sat upon its edge
I waited the miraculous flood, I waited
While the years passed and withered me away
I have snared the birds for food and eaten grass
And drunk the rain, and neither in dark nor shine
Wandered too for away to have heard the plash,
And yet the dancers have deceived me thrice
I have awakened from a sudden sleep
To find the stones were wet.

Young Man : My luck is strong
It will not leave me waiting, nor will they
That dance among the stones put me asleep
If I grew drowsy I can pierce my foot.

(p.213-14)

The dialogues differ in tone, The old man's speeches are not as highly pitched as are the speeches of Cuchulain who is confident and optimistic. The difference in tone reveals the ideological antagonism and its archetypal significance. The heroism of Cuchulain is foregrounded.

The songs of the musicians are different in language and verse form from the speeches of the old man and the young man. Yeats had felt that the heroes of Celtic mythology needed a different verse form than the blank verse of Renaissance. The imagination and culture of Irish men differed from European imagination and culture. Therefore, he created in his dance plays the form that varies blank verse with lyric metres. A lyrical passion runs through the musician's songs. The force has been imparted largely by a shortened poetic line which is simple in diction and structure. The complexity and archaisms of the pentametre are replaced by a simpler but stronger phrasing :

Young Man : Run where you will
Grey bird, you *shall* be perched upon my wrist
Some were called queens and yet have been
perched there.

First Musician : I have heard water plash; it comes, it comes
Look where it glitters. He has heard the plash
Look he has turned his head.

Musicians : He has lost what may not be found
Till men heap his burial mound
And all the history ends
He might have lived at his ease,
An old dog's head on his knees
Among his children and friends

(p. 217)

Young man's speech reveals his real interests. He has heard the water plash. But his mind is absorbed with the mystery of the hawk woman and a determination to subdue her. Immortality fades into insignificance when a more attractive field of war and victory presents itself before him. His real heroic self is betrayed by the use of *'shall'* that reveals stream determination to conquer the grey bird. His pursuit of the hawk woman does not bring any success to him. But he does not regret his efforts nor does he show any remorse for missing the water. Love and war are the real fields of his activity. Immortality does not have much charm. His emotions are involved in the search for mystery, Love and war.

Old Man : She has roused up the fierce woman of the hills
Aoife, and all her troops, to take your life,
And never till you are lying in the earth
Can you know rest

Young Man : The clash of war again !

(p.218)

The first exclamation we hand from him was at hearing the hawk woman's cry -

That cry !
There is that cry again. That woman made it
Bit why does she cry out as the hawk cries ?

(p. 215)

Mystery and war fascinate Cushulain -

I *will* face them
He comes : Cuchulain, son of Saultim comes.

(p. 218)

The hawk woman *'shall'* be perched on his wrist, he *will* face the warrior band of Aoife. A subtle play of shall/will and use of exclamations betray the real self of Cuchulain — the Irish hero, son of Saultim. Yeats' imagination could not stay for long in the abstract world of eternity. It is strongly fascinated by the life in this world with its ideas of love and war. Yeats is content of "lie down where all the ladden start/ In the foul rag and bone shop of the heart." The tone of dry intellectuality in the beginning of the play is replaced by more exuberant style of speech in the later part. This shift in the style of speech reveals Cuchulain's real self. His is not satisfied with the life 'among children and friends' — a simple, unheroic, monotonous existence. The final song of the musicians juxtaposes two styles of existence. One suggested by phrases like. 'human faces,' 'familiar memories', 'pleasant life' and another suggested by a different group of phrases like 'unmoistened eyes,' 'desolate places,' 'bitter life,' etc. Cuchulain had chosen the heroic path, being true to his inner self.

THE ONLY JEALOUSY OF EMER

Like *At the Hawk's Well* and unlike *On Baile's Strand, The Only Jealousy of Emer* was intended for an intellectually committed small group of audience. Elevation, not popularization, was its goal. Transitions between the worlds of daylight and dream — the mind awake and the mind in trance — are a characteristic feature of this play. The use of light and dark symbolism and differences in language and style enforce the two planes on which drama is staged. The action of the play shifts from human to superhuman and then to human plane of existence. The transition from the down- to-earth dialogue between Emer and Eithne Inguba in the beginning of the play to the elevated dialogue between human and supernatural between Emer and the Bricriu of the Sidhe is smoothly accomplished by a change of language and style. Then the drama is elevated to purely superhuman plane — dialogue between Cuchulain's ghost and woman of the Sidhe — through a still higher elevation of language and rhythm.

The dialogue between Emer and Eithne Inquaba is in a matter-of-fact style. Their language is simple and the register of language is ordinary speech and rhythms. The heroic blank verse is natural and flexible enough to carry out the various illocutionary needs of both Emer and Eithne Inquba. In the first place Emer persuades Eithne Inquba to call Cuchulain's spirit back from the world of dead. Eithne Inquba is hesitant in the beginning. But Emer provokes her with an urgency of tone to give up the formalities. Emer demands intensity and speed from Eithne Inquba's words. She persuades Eithne Inquba to speak in a more powerful manner.

Emer : Those words sound timidly; to be afraid
Because his wife is but three paces off.
When there is so great need, were but to prove
The man that chose you made but a poor choice
We're but two women struggling with the sea.

(p. 286)

Emer does not use many words but speaks realistically and puts forward bare facts. She leads Eithne Inquba to perform speech acts with greater force. Inquba's illocutions are successful, partially. Because Bricriu of the Sidhe takes possession of Cuchulain's body instead of his own spirit.

Such are the mysteries of the supernatural world that only Emer, not Ingube, can talk to Bricriu - 'maker of discord among gods and men.' Their dialogue demonstrate the interdependence and inter-penetration of the natural and the supernatural planes that was Yeats' primary belief. Bricriu of Sidhe has come to strike a bargain with Emer. Emer, being strong willed, does not recognise the power of the 'people of the wind' who, she thinks, 'are full of lying speech and mockery.' The supernatural is deglorified. Emer resents the attempts of Bricriu to force her make the deal. Till the very end Emer retaliates back the arguments of Bricriu. Their speeches are elevated in rhythm and diction though having flexibility at the same time that gives an effect of naturalness.

Figure of Cuchulain : A dream is body;
The dead move ever towards a dreamless youth
And when they dream no more return no more,
And those more holy shades that never lived
But visit you in dreams.

Emer : I know her sort
They find our men asleep, weary with war,
Lap them in cloudy hair or kiss their lips;
Our men awake in ignorance of it all,
But when we take them in our arms at night
We cannot break their solitude.

(p. 290)

Emer questions the ethos of supernatural and its interference in the world of human beings. The woman of Sidhe is near perfection and completion of her being. But Emer refers to her very slightingly — 'I know her sort' : She is contemptuous towards the agencies from the world on the other side of the grave because their intrucsion in human world defeats human goals and frustrates human hopes. She is truly heroic and sticks her ground till the very end in spite of the vehement illocutionary force of Bricriu's speeches.

Figure of Cuchulain : Cry out that you renounce his love;
make haste
And cry that you renounce his love for ever.

Emer : No, never will I give that cry

Figure of Cuchulain : Fool, Fool !
I am Fand's enemy come to thwart her will
And you stand gaping there. There is still time
Hear how the horses trample on the shore,
Hear how they trample /she has mounted up
Cuchulain's not beside her in the chariot.
There is still a moment left; cry out, cry out !
Renounce him and her power is at an end.
Cuchulain's foot is on the chariot steps
Cry -

Emer : I renounce Cuchulain's love for ever.

(p. 294)

A number of repetitions of phrases and words and exclamations combined with the vividly narrated dramatic style of Bricriu's speech win him renunciation of Cuchulain's love from Emer. Bricriu of the Sidhe performs excellent illocutionary acts and brings out his desired perlocutionary act. Emer is forced to change 'never' into 'for ever' just after a small ten line speech from Bricriu. The intense and elevated drama is followed by the moment of aesthetic calm. Cuchulain is restored to Eithne Inguba. The tragedy of Emer's destiny is brought into foreground by the single speech that Cuchulain — the human Cuchulain, is given at the end of the play. When Cuchulain returns back from his journey into the interior to the exterior day-light world he exclaims :

Your arms, your arms ! O Eithne Inguba
I have been in some strange place and am afraid.

(p. 294)

The simple speech with its brevity and passionate intensity seeking reassurance in human love reinforces the irony of Emer's fate. Cuchulain has renounced and rejected love of the superhuman and seeks comfort and security in the arms of his beloved. Yeats' protagonist values natural above the supernatural.

During his journey into the dark recesses of the soul Cuchulain connects with the figure representing perfection of soul. The superhuman, woman of Sidhe, is seen striving for human passions in the world of Yeats. The dialogue between the ghost of Cuchulain and woman of the sidhe elevates the play on a purely spiritual level. In the beginning of his career Yeats had worked with heroic register of language juxtaposing it beside lesser elevated styles of language. In this play he needed a register that would cut above heroic speech to record the intricacies of journeys into the innermost mysteries of the soul. He used shorter lines with more regular metre and approximate rhyme. The tetrameter lines are balanced by the frequent returns to a shorter line. And though the couplets rhyme, the sense units run beyond the couplets hinting at and balancing the superhuman stylization. The dance, woman of the Sidhe, suggests an unearthly moon-like beauty. The Ghost of Cuchulain is made to exclaim :

> Who is it stands before me there
> Shedding such light from limb and hair
> An when the moon, complete at last
> With every lapouring crescent past,
> And lonely will extreme delight,
> Flings out upon the fifteenth night ?
>
> (p. 291)

The beauty that looks perfect to the Ghost is not, somehow, complete; 'Because I long I am not complete'. Katharine worth caution's that "the audience in the theatre must feel the drawing power of the dancer and the hypnotic attraction of her dance but not be totally hyphotised,"[13] because complicated visual reactions are called for by the simultaneous presence of dream and waking worlds on the stage. There are communications taking place at various levels, at the same time. The woman of the Sidhe is shown luring Cuchulain away from her earthly memories and to unite with the more perfected creature — herself. She performs a number of illocutionary acts that build dramatic tension at this level. Unlike the speech acts of Bricriu, Fand Woman's speech acts are a failure, though her speeches are highly poetic and intense in rhythm.

Woman of the Sidhe : Could you that have loved many a woman
That did not reach beyond the human,
Lacking a day to be complete,
Love one that, though her heart can beat,
Lacks it by an hour or so ?

Ghost of Cuchulain : I know you now, not long ago
I met you on a cloudy hill
Beside old thorn tress and a well

A woman danced and a hawk flew,
I held out arms and hands; but you,
That now seem friendly, fled away,
Half woman and half bird of prey.

Woman of the Sidhe : Hold out your arms and hands again;
You were not so dumb founded when
I was that bird of prey, and yet
I am all woman now.

Ghost of Cuchulain : I am not
The young and passionate man I was,
And though that brilliant light surpass
All crescent forms, my memories
Weigh down my hands, abash my eyes.

(p. 292)

Woman of the Sidhe made an advance towards success in her illocutions. But Emer's timely decision frustrated her desire that had reached near fulfillment.

The play dramatized moments of intense emotional tremors ordered in a pattern of images and rhythms. The opening and the closing songs by the musicians establish the patterns and intensify the drama. The lyrics are in a highly elevated, philosophical register that elevates the play to a symbolic level. The lyrics provide clues for the play's symbolic meaning unfolding the real significance of its action. The rhythm is gradually built by repetitions of phrases and sentences and shortening and lengthening the lines.

O bitter reward
Of many a tragic tomb
And we though astonished are dumb
Or give but a sigh and a word
A passing word

(p. 295)

This stanzaic refrain in the final song is a plea for the tragic fate of the Fand woman. The rhythm and simplicity of this refrain account for its intensity and the play's appeal

THE DREAMING OF THE BONES

Like *At the Hawk's Well* and *The Only Jealousy of Emer*, the play is elevated in action, language and style. The action takes place on a supernatural plane. A pair of ghosts representatives of the mysteries of the dark interior of human nature are shown conversing with a young rebel who represents the daylight world of exterior reality. The action relates to Irish history. Diarmuid and Dervorgilla initiated the progressive disintegration of Ireland during its present cycle of two thousand years. Their spirits appear in the play before a young man who is committed to the cause of Irish freedom. The past and the present are juxtaposed. The ghost couple have been doing penance for seven hundred years. They need forgiveness of their crime in order to achieve expiation. They are seen persuading the young man to grant them forgiveness.

The ghost pair's speeches are in an elevated language. Their illocutions are full of pathos and remorse. Their words are very moving. There speeches are subjective and mysterious as contrasted with the objective and matter of fact style used by the young Man.

Young girl : Yes, Yes, I spoke
Of that most miserable, most accursed pair
Who sold their country into slavery, and yet
They were not wholly miserable and accursed
If somebody of their race, at last would say,
I have forgiven them.

Young man : O never, never
Small Diamond and Dervorgilla be forgiven

Young girl : If someone of their race forgave at last
Lip would be pressed on lip

Young man : O never, never
Shall Diarmind and Dervorgilla be forgiven

Young girl : Seven hundred years our lips have never met

Young man : Why do you look so strangely at one another ?
So strangely and so sweetly ?

Young girl : Seven hundred years

Young man : So strangely and so sweetly ....

(pp. 442-43)

The drama is taken to the height of a ritual. The lyrical chant intensifies the action. The speech — acts of the young girl gain force from the repetition of phrases. She has succeeded in gaining the young man's sympathy for their pathos. But sympathy is not followed by forgiveness. The youngman fights, with success, against the terrible temptation to yield to the illocutionary force of the ghost pair's speech acts. His sense of the wrong done by them to the people of Ireland leads him out of the trap. The lyrical rhythm of their dialogue intensifies the drama and carries it to the climax. The climax is reached, as usual, by shortening or lengthening the number of unstressed syllables as in the young man's speech at the top of the mountain.

So here we're on the summit. I can see
The Arian Islands, Connemara Hills,
And Galway in the breaking light; there too
The enemy has toppled roof and gable,
And torn the pavelling from ancient rooms;
What generations of old men had known
Like their own hands, and children wondered at,
Has boiled a trooper's porridge. That town had lain,
But for the pair that you would have me pardon,
Amid its gables and its battlements
Like any old admired Italian town.

(p. 443)

The young man's register of language is elevated. His syntax, diction and field of references are much above common speech. The elements of his language identify him with an intellectual principle of mind that he really is. He is a man of action or a modern Cuchulain.

The register of choral lyrics elevates the play even higher on the symbolic, poetic scale. The lyrics are refined and stylized by the use of interlocking rhyme.

Why does my heart beat so ?
Did not a shadow pass ?

It passed but a moment ago
Who can have trod in the grass ?

... (p. 433)

From 'Why does my heart beat so ?' to 'Why should the heart take fright ?' and from here to 'My heart ran wild when it heard,' the three lyrics with repetitions and subtle variations denote the progress in the drama. The beats are progressively intensified to mark an ascending movement. The opening song suggests the level at which the drama will be enacted. It expresses excitement and fear. The song's language is packed with images that suggest the significance of the play's action. The play's action consists of dreams and the images reveal the ecstatic nature of the dreams of dry bones which are

Like wine that fills to the top
A grey green cup of jade
Or may be an agate cup

(p. 434)

The occult symbolism is blended into the play's already exotic style that results in an excitement of language that brings it to the level of ritual of the soul.

The travel song divides the play in two distinct parts. The images of 'fouled well,' 'crying owl,' 'ragged thorn trees,' 'tomb nested owl,' ash, briar and thorn trees mark that the natural and the supernatural are interwoven. The epithets attached to the natural objects endow a mysticism to them. The refrain of the cock's crow calls out for the annunciation of a new cycle. The red cock of march is associated with spring and regeneration. The final lyric that winds up the plays sings the 'music of a lost kingdom' and cock's crow. The wild music at the end is stilled heralding a new dawn. The moment of transition has been realized in spite of the continuing penance of the dead bones. The historical cycle runs its course.

The three songs offer a coherent pattern of Yeats' themes. The play is remarkable for its brevity and well-knit structure. Richard Taylor thinks,

"One cannot help but admire the almost perfect construction of *The Dreaming of the Bones,* its clarity and brief intensity. Unlike the earlier

> dance plays, *The dreaming of the Bones* has a natural link with the real world of the audience and encourages their participation. Its success in terms of Yeats' development as a dramatist is in the precision with which the surface reality coincides with symbolic meaning and the boldness with which a drama of image, atmosphere and idea is expressed through lyrical patterning, rather than naturalistic plot sequences."[14]

The proximity of surface and symbolic meanings and lyrical pattering are the plays' strenghts.

CALVARY

From the very human figures of *The Dreaming of the Boned* Yeats jumps to the superhuman figure of Christ. In *Calvary* Christ dreams his passion through. It records the development of Christ, as a human being, as he moves through the last phases of his life cycle towards union with his opposite — himself as a God. A series of confrontations are presented to reveal aspects of his own self.

The chorus of musicians opens the plays with a highly symbolic song that elevates the play. The images of moon and heron relate to subjective natures in Yeats' system of beliefs. The compressed language and tetrameter verse rhythm distance the play from its overt meaning and suggest the deeper significance of the action. The first musician describes the scene before Christ's crucifixion that He dreams back. The mode of discourse is narrative. The direct narrative of the crowd and its mockery of Christ is a useful device that the playwright resorts to.

The first encounter of Christ is with Lazarus and the second with Judas. The beginnings of both are marked by intense lyrics. The speeches are colloquial, direct and modern in register. Only sometimes an occasional archaism or slightly stylized turn of phrase elevates the language. The simplicity of language signifies lack of grandeur in the figure of God. Yeats is heading towards a heretical interpretation of the concept of Godhead. Yeats brings Godhead down to the very human level. Neither Lazarus nor Judas want to recognize Christ's power over their lives. Christ's illocutions fail to convince them of His control over the world and its people. They betrayed Christ in order to prove their freedom.

Judas : That was they very thought that drove me wild
I could not bear to think you had but to whistle
And I must do; but after that I thought
Whatever man betrays Him will be free

(p. 454)

Not even the Roman soldiers, the dice players, recognize His power. Their language is even more simple and down to earth.

First Roman soldier - They say you're good and that you made the world
But that's no matter.

Their definition of God robs Christ of his cloak of grandeur. They do not need Him

First Roman soldier - One thing is plain
To know that he has nothing that we need
Must be a comfort to Him.

(p.456)

The symbolism of the play foregrounds the objective loneliness of Christ. 'God did not die for the heron,' as the refrain in the first song makes clear; he did not appear to the birds, as revealed in the final song; and he is not needed for anything by the Roman soldiers as well, Feeling so utterly rejected from every corner Christ cries in agony.

'My father, why hast thou forsaken me ?'

Christ is human to the very core of his being. It seems as if Yeats left nothing but capital 'H' to make 'Him' God.

A FULL MOON IN MARCH

Before writing *A Full Moon in March* Yeats had written a number of prose plays that we have kept out of the scope of our thesis. *Calvary* was the last of his plays for dancers. But *The King of the Great Cloak Tower* and *A Full Moon in March* are the plays truly inspired by and intended to be enacted by dancers. Therefore, though not published as plays for dancers, they belong to the phase of dance plays.

Yeats is pushing his elevated, symbolic drama towards anti-illusionism. He puts emphasis upon the element of artifice in his plays. The attendants in *A Full Moon in March* open the play casually tailing about their roles in the play and discussing about the song that they will sing. Later in the play they are performing the roles of different characters –– the severed Head, the King, the captain of the Guard. The play is overtly anti-naturalist in its techniques.

In the use of modern idiom Yeats shows as much creativity as he did in the use of peasant dialect in the plays that belong to the first phase of his career. The speeches in this play are enlivened by an interplay and opposition of registers rhythms, and sound patternings. The language of this play looks forward to the more realistic style of *The Herne's Egg* and *Purgatory*. The character antagonism between the severed head and the Queen is projected in terms of language too.

The Swine herd :	The beggars of my country say that he That sings you best shall take you for a wife
The Queen :	He that best sings his passion
The Swine herd :	And they say The kingdom is added to the gift
The Queen :	I swore it
The Swine herd :	But what if some blind aged cripple sing Better than wholesome men ?
The Queen :	Some I reject Some I have punished for their impudence None I abhor can sing
The Swine herd :	So that's the catch Queen look at me, look long at these foul rags, At hair more foul and regged than my rags. Look on my scratched foul flesh. Have I not come Through dust and mire ? There is the dust and mire Beasts scratched my flesh; my memory too is gone, Because great solitudes have driven me mad.

(p. 623)

The queen speaks an elevated archaic register. Her speeches are formal in tone. The Swineherd often speaks a colloquial modern register which is awkward in its syntax. The blank verse is adapted to suit the cadences of contemporary speech. By this method of using language Yeats projects his metaphysical vision which reconciles the anti-theses of temporal and spiritual male and female, war and love, as well as providing an analogue of poetic creation. The conflict proceeds at a fast pace which is intensified and accelerated further by the lyrics that punctuate the dialogues.

The play has a pronounced ritual form from the beginning that lead to the performance of the central ritual at the end of the play. The queen performs the ritual dance accompanied by highly elevated symbolic songs. The severed head of the Swineherd sings. Song, music and dance are combined to enact the moment of reconciliation of opposites. The whole play has been an elaborate structure of the symbolic conflict of contraries. The Swineherd's illocutions to win over the Queen did not succeed till after his head, the severed head, sang. His illocutions were too direct and offending in their style and tone to get the intended result. But after he was beheaded his head sang the Jack and Jill nursery rhyme with significant variations of content and rhyme. After the song the Queen is won over. She performs a dance that grows quicker as the moment of reconciliation approaches nearer. The climax is reached in terms of music, song, dance and rhythm. It is followed by an aesthetic lull. The play ends with a song that transforms the particular into general and archetypal. The song is highly exalted in tone and rhythm as it sings of the ecstasy of unification.

THE KING OF THE GREAT CLOCK TOWER

The play marks a high point of achievement in Yeats' experiments with the form of dance drama. The play was 'magnificently acted and danced' as Yeats wrote to Olivia Shakespeare. Elevation popularization poles were successfully fused in the form. The play marked a high degree of stylization and proved theatrically 'most effective'. Ninette de Valois, the popular dancer, acted and danced the Queen's part. As the would not speak dialogues the conflict between the queen and the stroller could not be presented sharply. To depict the antagonism between the opposing principles in nature Yeats wrote *A Full Moon in March. The king of the Great Clock Tower* was first written in prose. Yeats had rewritten it in verse after having written the next play - *A Full Moon in March.* The two plays have much in common.

The dialogues are in a modern and colloquial register of language.

The Stroller : Enough that I am called
A stroller and a fool. That you are called
King of the Great Clock Tower

The King : What do you want ?

The Stroller : A year ago I heard a brawler say
That you had married a woman called
Most beautiful of her sex. I am a poet
From that day out I put her in my songs.
And day by day she grew more beautiful.
Hard hearted men that plough the earth and sea
Sing what I sing, yet I that sang her first
Have never seen her face.

The King : Have you no wife
Mistress of friend to put into a song ?

The Stroller : I had a wife. The image in my head
Made her appear fat, slow, thick of the limbs,
In all her movements like a Michaelmas goose.
I left her, but a night or two ago
I ate my sausage at a tavern table —
A stroller and a man of no account
I dine among the ganders — a gander scoffed,
Said I would drink myself to sleep, or cry
My head among the dishes on the table,
Because of a woman I had never seen.

(p. 635)

The conversation between the King and the Stroller has actual speech rhythms. The speeches of the Stroller preserve the casualness and abruptness of the common speeches even while describing his spiritual vision.

The Stroller : I ran to the Boyne Water
And there a sea-mew and the salt sea-wind

Yelled Godhead, on a round green hillock lay,
Nine days I fasted there — but that's a secret
Between us three — then Aengus and the Gods
Appeared, and when I said what I had sworn
Shouted approval. Then great Angus spoke —
O listen, for I speak his very words —
On stroke of midnight when the old year dies,
Upon that stroke, the tolling of the bell,
The Queen shall kiss your mouth — his very
 words —
Your Queen, my mouth, the Queen shall kiss
 my mouth.

(p. 637)

The verbs like 'yelled' and 'shouted' are used in the context of godhead. It has a startling effect. But it is quite consistent with Yeats' ideological framework. The human and the superhuman, in Yeats, are brought to exist on a single plane. The language that describes spiritual vision is the language of common use. The poet's drunken oath and images of geese and genders are equivalent to the mystical prophecy of the holy man. His illocutions are, like the illocutions of the Swineherd in *A full Moon in March,* direct and abrupt. He does not perform illocutionary acts. He declares the perlocutionary acts that the Queen is destined to perform.

The antagonism between the Queen and the Stroller is brought into foreground through the songs — its images and rhythms. The songs of the Stroller are cast in free verse form based on tetrameters. The Queen's songs are in strict trimeter for maximum impact.

The Queen : He longs to kill
My body until
That sudden shudder
And limbs are still

O what may come
Into my womb,
What caterpillar
My beauty consume ?

(p. 638)

The song juxtaposes creation and destruction in an extremely condensed language. The vocabulary recalls the poem *'Leda and the Swan'* as does the theme. The songs of the king and the Stroller and their alternative verse forms emphasize the symbolic antagonism which is more sharply presented in *A Full Moon in March.*

The songs lead to the dance which marks the climactic point of the drama. Yeats brings dance into full symbolic significance. The ritual dance of the Queen before the severed head increases in frenzy as the music picks up momentum. At the stroke of mid-night the timeless and the temporal are united. The opposites are reconciled. She sings and presses her lips on the lips of the severed head. It is a moment of annihilation as well as creation. The moment of unification dissolves into a standstill. Frenzy leads to calm and quiet. The play is elevated to its highest plane in the creation of an unearthy atmosphere that dissolves into a vision of pure spirit. The climax is reached in terms of imagery, sound, rhythm, and movement. The linguistic resources and theatrical techniques are unified into a single pattern to foreground the mysterious nature of human soul.

THE HERNE'S EGG

In his dance plays Yeats presented minimum characters and scenes concentrating on moments of intense experiences of spiritual nature. The language was highly elevated, symbolic and condensed, marked by lyrical intensity. Yeats had pushed the elevation motive too far to maintain it for long. The plays were a success in terms of Yeats' ideal of drama. But by their very nature they were neither intended to nor did reach a popular audience. As a dramatist Yeats could not, for long, suppress his craving for a larger audience. He felt a compelling need to widen the gyre.

The Herne's Egg marks a significant move into the direction of pupularization. Instead of presenting a single opposition of universal forces and their reconciliation Yeats attempts a new departure in *The Herne's Egg.* He deviates from his theory of minimalism and austerity. A variety of ideas, images, language styles and verse forms are integrated into a single dramatic whole. The patterns are equally personal but more elaborate and complex.

The songs and dialogues in this play do not have different styles. The songs are not elevated in language or lyricism. Metrical regularity is not maintained. There are irregularities and mixing of various types at every level. The play is based on a tragi-comic vision that is reflected in language too. The verse forms of dialogues range from trimestres to pentametres with a marked irregularity of use that is informal and punctures the elevation that is promised by the ideas.

Congal : Women thrown into despair
By the winter of their virginity
Take its abominable snow,
As boys take common snow, and make
An image of God or bird or beast
To feed their sensuality
Ovid had a literal mind,
And though he sang it neither knew
What lonely lust dragged down the gold
That crept on Danae's lap, no knew
What rose against the moony feathers
When Ledalay upon the grass.

(p. 649)

The metrical irregularity may give a touch of mockery to the seriousness which the context demands.

Like the verse forms, syntax too is mixed. Colloquialism, repetitions and exclamations are found side by side with poetic elevation and lyrical rhythm. The idiom is throughout modern and charged that adds to the naturalness and excitement of the tragi-comic tone of the play.

Congal - I am king Congal of Connacht and of Tara,
That wise, victorious, voluble, unlucky,
Blasphemous, famous, infamous man
Fool, take this spite when red with blood
Show it to the people and get all the pennies;
What does it matter what they think ?
The Great Herne knows that I have won.

(p. 676)

The language of Congal is the language of the hero and of the fool. The antinomies are reconciled in his own self. He deflates the tragic implications of his death by speaking of it in a casual manner and by not trying to defend his life. Heroic is rendered mock-heroically following the mood of the entire play. The play is

Yeats' mockery of his won elevated ideas, serious philosophy that he expounded with a solemn gravity in the earlier plays. The play is an aesthetic mask of the serious philosophy.

> Corney : King Congal must be born a donkey !
>
> Attracta : Because we were not quick enough.
>
> Corney : I have heard that a donkey carries its young
> Longer than any other beast,
> Thirteen months it must carry it.
> (He laughs)
> All that trouble and nothing to show for it,
> Nothing but just another donkey.
>
> (p. 678)

The songs are neither heavily symbol laden nor stylized. Corney's song 'this they nailed upon a post' is a direct exposition of ideas. It is written in a ballad form of uneven line lengths, awkward rhythms and equally awkward couplet rhymes. Attracta's song 'When I take a beast to my joyful heart' too uses a ballad form. Ballad form has all the advantages of popularization and an air of romanticism about it that is very congenial to Yeats' taste.

PURGATORY

Unlike the mythic hero Cuchulain of some of his later plays, this plays takes anti-heroic figures as protagonist — 'a silly old man' and his 'loutish son.' The action is simple and concentrated. Yeats presents the same philosophy of inter-relationship between the supernatural and the natural. In his system the bonds of passion that are formed in the temporal world are shown to last even in the world of supernatural as in *The Dreaming of the Bones*. *'Purgatory'* doesn't purge but renews the passion and adds to the 'complexities of mire and blood.'

The language of the play shows a gradual shift from elevated, formal register to a colloquinal, harsh register in the speeches of the old man. The old man is calm and controlled in the beginning of the play. His language too is elegant and formal.

They had loved the trees that he cut down
To pay what he had lost at cards
Or spent on horses, drink and women,
Had loved the house, had loved all
The intricate passages of the house
Where great men grew up, married, died.
I here declare a capital offense.

(p. 683)

The speech is measured and regular in rhythm. At other places his speeches acquire harsh tones with the change of subject.

I have the education that befits
A bastard that a pedlar got
Upon a tinker's daughter in a ditch

(p. 684)

The natural, colloquial words and the breath taking pace reproduce contemporary speech pattern. The speech rhythms of the old man move towards higher irregularity as his passions are worked up. He is deeply obsessed by the sufferings of his dead parents. He shows a close and deep feeling for them unlike his son whose attitude shows detachment. His speeches continue on and on in thought and tone without heeding to the interruptions from the boy. His sobriety in the beginning gives way to vehement emotions and his wits begin to wander.

My father and my son on the same jock knife !
That finishes - there - there - there
Hush - a - bye baby, they father's a knight
Thy mother a lady, lovely and bright
No. that's something I read in a book
And if I sing it must be to my mother
And I lack rhyme.

(p. 688)

In his frenzy he kills his son and is bewildered by his own passion. As soon as the son dies his father and mother, previously 'pedlar' and 'tinker's daughter' are transformed into 'knight' and 'lady.' His lack of remorse for killing his son reveals his detachment to the present as his son showed for the past. He is happy for his parents because he thinks he has put an end to their suffering. But their dream returns and the futility of his efforts is proved to him. The same pathetic realization dawns upon him that has been laughed away in *The Herne's Egg* by Corney — 'All that troubles and nothing to show for it/Nothing but just another donkey.' In the present play Yeats could not mock at it. He accepts the reality with the sobriety of an old man. As the wildness cools down the language again is refined and rhythm mounts to lyricism.

O God
Release my mother's sould from its dream !
Mankind can do no more. Appease
The misery of the living and the remorse
of the the dead.

(p. 689)

The terms like 'appease' and 'remorse' enter Yeats' idiolect as he matures. The last line of the dialogue is a wide generalisation. Yeats moves from particular to archetypal and general.

The language of the body also shows a variety. It varies from broad dialect to completely natural and grammatically correct phrasing. In the beginning he speaks in an ungrammatical language.

Boy - half door - hall door
Higher and thither day and night,
Hill or hollow, shouldering this pack,
Hearing you talk

(p. 681)

He speaks in a grumbling tone. The accumulation of predicates without a subject conveys the exasperation of the boy. The apparent lack of links between sentences carries a weight of emotions and shows his self-absorption. He is engrossed within his own self. He does not show any interest in his father's story. The tone of antagonism between father and son is quite unmistakable. His father too is absorbed in himself. Both are alienated from each other. At one point it grows intolerable to the body.

Body : I have had enough !
Talk to the jack daws if talk you must

(p. 682)

The exclamation, the imperative and the archaic inversion complete the process of alienation between the two. The boy is not in the least sympathetic towards his father and is completely disinterested in the past.

THE DEATH OF CUCHULAIN

In an entirely different purgatory we find Cuchulain dreaming back the passionate moments of his life in the world of Yeats' poetic drama. *The Death of Cuchulain* marks the finale of Yeats' dramatic creation. To wind up the sago of Cuchulain the main events of his life are re-encountered. The moments return one by one with a significant change of attitude. Cuchulain is standing at the threshold of this world. he is about to cross the boundary line between the natural, human world of passionate, heroic existence and the superhuman, abstract world at the other side of the grave. His attitude is one of detachment and calm. He encounters various phases in the development of his personality in the form of Eithne Inguba, Aoife, and the blind man — characters from the earlier plays.

The play is a king of winding up of the story. The language is free of archaisms of obvious poeticisms. The idiom, syntax and rhythm are natural and simple. Sense units and lines coincide.

Cuchulain : You thought that if you changed I'd kill you for it
When everything sublunary must change,
And If I have not changed that goes to prove
That I am monstrous.

Eithne Inguba : You're not the man I loved
That violent man forgave no treachery
if thinking what you think you can forgive
It is because you are about to die.
(p. 697)

The style of speech remains formal and single throughout except for the long speech of the blind man. The blind man's dialogue is as informal and irregular as his ideas.

Blind man : They say that you are weak with wounds
I stood between a fool and the sea at Baile's strand
When you went mad. What's bound about your hands ?
So that they cannot move ? Some womanish stuff.
(p. 701)

His thoughts suddenly change and sentences break abruptly. He is the anti-heroic figure opposed to Cuchulain — the legendary hero. Cuchulain speaks an elegant, rhythmic language —

There floats out there
The shape that I shall take when I am dead,
My soul's first shape, a soft feathery shape
And is not that a strange shape for the soul
Of a great fighting man ?

(p. 702)

The final self-interrogation marks the abrupt break of the tone of interiorisation. He was lost in a reverie but the final question seems are much a self-interrogation as a rhetorical question addressing and involving the audience across the stage. Yeats is reaching at once to the inner mind of the protagonist as well as the minds of the audience.

REFERENCES :

Note : All the quotations from the plays refer to the Collected Plays of W.B. Yeats.

1. A. Normal Jeffares and A.S. Knowland, *A commentary on the Collected Plays of W.B. Yeats,* pp. 55-56.
2. W.B. Yeats, *Essays and Introductions,* p. 256.
3. W.B. Yeats, *Letters,* ed. A. Wade, p. 460.
4. B. Rajan, *W.B. Yeats : A Critical Introduction,* p. 159.
5. W.B. Yeats, *Four Play for Dancers,* p. 56.
6. W.B. Yeats, *Essary and Introductions,* p. 166.
7. *Ibid.*, p. 170.
8. *Ibid.*, p. 159.
9. Katharine Worth, *The Irish Drama of Europe from Yeats to Beckett,* p. 4.
10. Martha Johnso, 'Reflections of Inner Life : Masks and Masked acting in Ancient Greek Tragedy and Japanese Noh Drama', *Modern Drama,* XXXV, 1 (March 1992).
11. Denis Donogue, *The Third Voice : Modern British and Verse Drama,* p. 53..
12. B. Rajan, *W.B. Yeats : A Critical Introduction,* p. 58.
13. Katharine Worth, *The Irish Drama of Europe from Yeats to Beckett,* p. 168.
14. Richard Taylor, *The Drama of W.B. Yeats : Irish Myth and the Japanese Noh,* p. 155.

Chapter Four

Reaching Into the Silence : The Plays of T.S. Eliot

Words, after speech reach
Into the silence. Only by the form, the pattern,
Can words or music reach
The stillness.

(V'Burnt Norton' *Four Quarters*)

The present interpretation of Eliot's poetic drama, like the study of Yeats' drama, will bear out the aims and ideology of the writer in the selection, combination, variation and creative uses of language — language in its multilevel form and twentieth century perspective that treats language as being functional and dynamic.

Eliot undertook play writing when he was requested to write a drama for the Canterbury Festival of June 1935. Therefore, he set on his adventurous journey with a restricted field of discourse and a limited scope of audience. The result was the creation of *Murder in the Cathedral.* It proved successful in attaining its limited objective. But Eliot was not satisfied. He realised that the audiences who attended his play come "to be patiently bored and to satisfy themselves with the feeling that they have done something meritorious."[1] Katharine Worth argues that "his anxiety to make contact with 'real' audiences was an important factor in the evolution of his post-war style. He put the poetry on a thin diet and overlaid his symbols with a conventionally seductive facade."[2]

Out interpretation of Eliot's poetic drama will trace the evolution of Eliot's language and style in relation to his increasing desire for popularization. There was a 'prudent devil' in Eliot that guided him during his dramatic 'pilgrimage.' We will examine how it influenced certain aspects of his language. Still, our analysis will discover that the basic tenets of his philosophy are never lost sight of. The various levels of language use as in Yeats — do not fail to distinguish the 'real' from the 'mask.' He will also find out the way the 'mask' affects the fulfilment of the basic motive behind his revival of poetic drama : whether his experiments lead him towards a balancing of the two gyres, as in Yeats, or whether he is forced to contract the elevation gyre in his over enthusiasm to expand the circle of the audience which we suspect to be the case with him.

MURDER IN THE CATHEDRAL

Unlike Yeats who aimed at a 'profane perfection of mankind' Eliot never questioned the primacy of the super-natural world over the natural world. The supernatural was essentially religious for Eliot whereas it was a world of mysterious, spiritual beings which were secular for Yeats. The definition of the supernatural world differs as do the ideologies of Yeats and Eliot. Yeats chose his protagonists from old myths or legends. Eliot takes a saint as the protagonist in *Murder in the Cathedral.* The play was written for the Canterbury festival of June 1935 which is responsible for the choice of Thomas Becket and his martyrdom as the subject of the play. It also confirms Eliot's complete transformation from agnosticism to Christianity. The play enacts a conflict between the material and the spiritual worlds. The conflict takes place in the Archbishop's mind.

Thomas Becket — the Archbishop — stands at the pinnacle of existence. He is spiritually awakened. He returns to England after living in exile for seven years. He appears on the stage with a speech of paradoxical statements, abstract imagery and cryptic phrases.

> You know and do not know, that it is to act or suffer
> You know and do not know, that action is suffering
> And suffering action. Neither does the agent suffer
> Nor the patient act. But both are fixed

In an eternal action, an eternal patience
To which all must consent that it may be willed
And which all must suffer that they may will it
That the pattern may subsist, the the wheel
may turn and still
Be for ever still (p. 17)

The language of the dialogue suggests a struggle with words to express the vision of an awakened sensibility. The paradoxical pair of positive and negative — know, do not know; a pair of words — action and suffering; pair of alternative patterns of active and passive voice — that it may be willed / that they may will it; and finally the pun upon the word 'still' are instrumental in the communication of meaning. Paradoxical statements are essential to reveal the nuances of spiritual reality. The chorus women typify the dualism of eternity and time, duration and flux, spirit and flesh, action by suffering and suffering by action. The Archbishop 'knows' what men do not, Action / suffering pair is turned and tossed in various contexts and different parts of speech to convery the oneness of them. In a stroke of dramatic irony Eliot makes the fourth tempter repeat the same action — suffering speech. He throws Becket's words back at him. The Crchbishop grows to martyrdom before our own eyes. The process of his spiritual progress includes learning the true meaning of his own words and putting it into action. This is the crux of drama that is enacted on the Archbishop's soul. The speech becomes a crucial speech act when used by the tempter. It brings about, successfully, the desired effect. The Archbishop them 'knows,' truly, what other people do not. He learns that it is essential to merge one's will into the will of God. One cannot even will to be a martyr. The murder of the Archbishop is the physical manifestation of this process.

The action-suffering motif combined with the wheel-still point image expresses the spiritual vision of Eliot. The vision consists of the relationship between temporal and eternal worlds. The temporal world is a whirlpool of action and suffering. The pattern repeats itself again and again. The life of the Archbishop has been no exception. When he discovers it he is horrified.

Can I neither act, nor suffer
Without predication ?

In glorifying himself for the honour of martyrdom the Archbishop has been defeating his own end. The Fourth tempter makes him realize the need to fight against the temptation of willing martyrdom. While he fights 'the intractable tide' of his ambition the Priests and the women of Canterbury plead with him. The whole atmosphere is charged with excitement and fear.

And the earth presses up against our feet
What is the sickly smell, the vapour ?
The earth is heaving to parturition of issue of hell
What is the sticky dew that forms
on the back of my hand ?

The sensuousness of imagery vividly describes the horror of the chorus women. The Archbishop is their saviour. His sacrifice is essential, otherwise hell becomes a poignant reality :

God is leaving us, God is leaving us, more pang
more pain the birth or death
Sweet and cloying, through the dark air
Falls the stifling scent of despair;
The forms take shape in the dark air;
Puss-purr or leopard, footfall of padding bear,
Palm-pat of nodding ape, square hyaena waiting
For laughter, laughter, laughter. The Lords of hell are here
They curl round you, lie at your feet, writing and
swing through the dark air,
O Thomas Archbishop, save us, save us, save us,
save yourself that we may be saved
Destroy yourself and we are destroyed.

(pp. 29-30)

They sense the battle waging in the Archbishop's mind. Their fear mounts to panic at the thought of the triumph of evil. The hellish beasts are vividly depicted. The precise movements are recorded to make the picture of hell palpable. The chant amounts to a ritual. The persuasions of the chorus women and the priests are successful. The Archbishop will no more be tempted 'to do the right deep for the wrong reason.' He will 'lay down his life for the sheep.' The tempters failed in their speech-acts. They could not lure the Archbishop to material life or willing martyrdom. He emerged triumphant out of the trap after a long, deep silence into which he fell for sometime. The still point of the wheel stopped. His stillness or calm is juxtaposed against the hysterical restlessness of the tempters, priests and the chorus women.

The fear of damnation is replaced by the fear for Archbishop's life. His life is in danger. The danger becomes oppressive. As the danger approaches nearer the senses are quickened and activated. the chorus women hear strange voices, see strange movements, smell and taste strange things :

> I have smelt them, the death bringers,
> The death bringers, senses are quickened
> By subtle forebodings; I have heard
> Fluting in the night time, fluting and owls,
> have seen at noon
> Scaly wings slanting over, huge and ridiculous,
> I have tasted
> The savour of purified flesh in the spoon I have felt
> The hearing of death at nightfall, restless absurd.
>
> (p. 41)

The approaching danger makes them hyper-sensitive. They feel guilty as the crime is committed before their eyes. Whenever evil deeds are committed the whole universe takes part in it. The women of Canterbury feel themselves to be a part of the crime. They feel guilty of inaction. Fear, suspicion, guilt, evil pervade the whole atmosphere.

Passivity is deep-rooted in the characters of Eliot. As already pointed out during our interpretation of Yeats' *The Countess Cathleen,* the language of evil is the language of negation— negation at different levels of language, from morphological to syntactic, and semantic levels.[2] Evil, that pervades the whole of the play, is present in the form of negation at all these levels of language. At the morphological level we have items with the negative prefix un - and in - : the chorus women lived 'preferring to pass un̲observed'; they believed, 'Dentiny waits in the hand of God, shaping the still un̲shapen; they know of 'minor in̲justices' and girls that 'dis̲appeared un̲accountably'; their 'brains un̲skinned'; the Four Tempters tell Thomas 'All things are un̲real.' At the level of semantics too there are abundant vocabulary items like fear, danger, ill, evil, violence, duplicity, illusions, despise, oppression, scandals, enemies, disease, passivity, deception, dark, traitor, horror, etc. And we have already discussed the speech acts of the tempters and the knights which are exercises in negation : the force of their illocutions is directed towards making Thomas do something that does not conform with his purpose. At the interactive speech level evil manifests itself in the form of efforts to deceive or dissuade the listener. And 'good' manifests itself in the form of persuasion that directs the choice of the listener in the right direction as the chorus, the priests do. Such linguistic manifestations of the theme of good and evil elevate the drama to the levels of religious and spiritual existence.

The weather imagery communicates the fear of action and love of inaction in the choric onlookers. When the Archbishop returns the people of Canterbury fear

> ... disturbance of quiet seasons :
> Winter shall come bringing death from the sea,
> Ruinous spring shall beat at our doors,
> Root and shoot shall eat our eyes and our ears,
> Disastrous summer burn up the beds of our stream
> And the poor shall wait for another decaying October.
> Why should the summer bring consolation
> For Autumn fires and winter fogs ?
> What shall we do in the heat of summer
> But wait in barren orchards for another October ?
>
> (p. 12)

The quint essential Eliot characters wait for winter — a season of death and decay. The return of Thomas would mean a shedding of spiritual lethargy — a painful activity for them. They donot want to disturb the quiet rhythms of their lives — living and partly living. The rhetorical questions add force to their efforts to resist the coming of summer. They feel the change with all vehemence.

Eliot was a critic of secular ideas. He felt the whole of the contemporary literature corrupted by secularism. When the secular ideals become dominant, crimes like murder of the Archbishop are committed. Such sins pollute every particle of existence. The chorus gives an anguished cry :

> Clear the air ! clear the sky ! wash the wind !
> Take stone from stone and wash them
> The land is foul, the water is foul, our beasts and
> ourselves defiled with blood
> We are soiled by a filth that we cannot clean, united to
> supernatural vermin,
> It is not we alone, it is not the house, it is not the
> city that is defiled,
> But the world that is wholly foul.
>
> (p. 47)

The very elements of life are stained with blood. The three exclamations and the tone of urgency convey that corruption is thorough. The secular world preoccupied with its concern for power in material terms could not see that 'the church is stronger for this action.' The Third Priest realises the truth. The Chorus sings thanks to God for giving another saint to Canterbury :

> Even in us the voices of seasons, the snuffle of winter
> The song of spring, the drone of summer, the voices of
> beasts and of birds, praise Thee.
>
> (p. 53)

The images of seasons, beasts and birds are reemphasised at the end. They have been active participants in the drama and offer their thanks through the chorus.

The knights speak their apologies after the murder. Their speeches are put in prose. They address the audience directly. Eliot is trying to have that active participation of the audience for which he envied the music-hall comedian. The knights speak a language of political expediency. The shift of mode from poetry to prose is meant to shock the audience out of their complacency.

The knights entered the stage in a hostile context and their speeches are a culmination of that opposition and hostility that surrounded them. Their speeches are short and snappy.

> First knight : Not for today, but matters urgent
> Have brought us from France, we rode hard
> Took ship yesterday, landed last night,

Having business with the Archbishop.

(p. 31)

The sentence structure, phrases and tone convey their prejudices and hostility. While trying to persuade the Archbishop into submission to the king their tone is resentful and arrogant. It defeats their own ends. Their speech-acts and style of speech does not conform with their desired perlocutionary effect. Hence they fail in their illocutions. They seem to have come with a decision and found and excuse to perform the evil deed. They are not men of words but of swords. Their words did not succeed. They wish to execute their task with swords :

Second knight : Enough of words

Four knights : We come for the king's justice
We come with swords

(p. 41)

The knights' lyric 'come down Daniel' is written in allusion to a jazz rhythm by American poet Vachel Lindsay called 'Daniel Jazz' published in 1920. Eliot takes a form of entertainment and explores the benefits it could yield to his poetic drama.

The jazz rhythms lead to a blood and death speech from the Archbishop —

No traitor to the king, I am a priest,
A Christian, saved by the blood of Christ
Ready to suffer with my blood
This is the sign of the Church always
The sign of blood. Blood for blood.
His blood given to buy my life,
My blood given to pay for his death,
My death for his death.

(p. 46)

Thomas is preparing himself for the bloody act. When called a traitor again and again, he is provoked. The word 'traitor' is unjust for him. The great Archbishop becomes furious and retaliates :

Knights : Traitor ! Traitor ! Traitor !

Thomas : You, Reginaled, three times traitor you :
Traitor to me as my temporal vassel
Traitor to me as your spiritual lord,

Traitor to God in desecrating his Church.

(p. 47)

The missing linking verb, repetition of the pronoun 'you,' a paradigm of predicates convey his fury and the sense of injustice. It is a rare moment when we get a glimpse of the human being hidden behind the great stature of the Archbishop — a would be martyr. He has evolved spiritually, defeating various temptations.

Mr. Martin Brown interprets the tempters as 'the interlocutors' whom Elite needed 'to make dramatic dialogue.'[4] Eliot is reaching to the roots of drama — presenting inner conflict, different levels of action, distinct groups of characters. The presentation is invariably in the context of religion.

The reinstate poetry on the stage Eliot creates structural or dramatic rhythms. There are four tempters to stage the inner conflict of Becket's mind. There are as many knights to carry out the climactic act of murder. The Tempters kill the ego, the 'I' in the Archbishop. The knights put an end to his 'temporal vessel'. The final victory belongs to the Archbishop himself. He is the martyr — the Saint. Spirituality is paradoxical, it eludes expression as well as understanding.

The tempters represent the weaknesses of Thomas as the knights represent evil in the outside world. The tempters are men of words. They use rhetorical style of speech. Their tone of allurement is contrasted with the knight's tone —

First temper : Your lordship won't despise an old friend out
of favour ?
Old Tom, gay Tom, Becket of London,
Your lordship won't forget that evening on
the river
When the king and you and I were all friends
together ?
Friendship should be more than bitting Time
can sever
What, my lord, now that you recover
Favour with the king, shall we say that
summer's over
Or that the good time cannot last ?

(p. 18)

The negative rhetorical questions of the First Tempter do not move the Archbishop. The second Tempter unfolds a positive bait :

Second Tempter : Think, my Lord,
Power obtained grows to glory
Life lasting, a permanent possession
A templed tomb, monument of marble
Rule over men reckon no madness

Thomas : To the man of God what gladness ?

Tempter : Sadness
Only to those giving love to God alone
Shall he who held the solid substance
Wander waking with deceitful shadows ?
Power is present. Holiness hereafter.

(p. 20)

The continuous rhyme — madness, gladness, sadness — endows a chant-like smoothness to the dialogue. He enumerates the enchantments of power and the glory that power leads to. But the determination of the Archbishop is strong. The Third Tempter offers treason to the King. Thomas is quick to retort back :

And if the Archbishop cannot trust the king
How can he trust those who work for king's undoing?

(p. 24)

His 'will is hard to bend.' It is indomitable. The Fourth Tempter is the very self to Thomas. His tone, his words are ambiguous. He repeats the action-suffering speech that the Archbishop had delivered to the priests and chorus women. The speech is not changed in the least. But the context transforms the whole meaning. Repetition in Eliot always implies ironic complications. Here, the context further complicates the already complex speech. The protagonist is going through a process of self-discovery. The focus of the drama shifts to the soul of the Archbishop. The climax is reached. The realization that he has to translate his teachings into action dawns upon archbishop. The illocutions of the Fourth Tempter are the illocutions of his own soul. The process of self discovery runs parellel to the process of learning the meaning of martyrdom. He discovers the question and then looks for an answer. The Further Tempter leads him to the discovery of the question. The

Tempters, The Priests, the women of Canterbury combine their efforts to hasten the discovery of an answer. The drama is elevated to the level of a ritual — chant by the dialogues of the three groups of helpers. The moment of final revelation occurs after a long pause on the part of Thomas. The silence meanwhile enhances the significance of his decision. Words and silence both play significant roles in taking the drama to the spiritual plane of existence. The combined illocutionary force of the three groups was needed to bring about the perlocutionary effect the poet wished to.

The groups characters — chorus in the form of the women of Canterbury and semi-chorus in the form of Priests, Tempters and Knights play an important role in the play as they make the crucial action take place. The women of Canterbury speak the dialogues and sing in groups, whereas the Priests, Tempters and Knights play individual roles ad well as group roles.

The women of Canterbury use a suggestive style of language : they whisper secrets and murmur their fears about the fate of Canterbury. They are omniscient and speak or sing aloud their knowledge. They give the audience sovereign knowledge of the past and also tell them their forebodings of fear and danger in future. Their language activity forms a significant part of the play. Their self-interrogations in the beginning of the play lead and unearthly feeling to the drama.

> "Are we drawn by danger ? Is it the knowledge of safety,
>   that draws our feet
> Towards the Cathedral ? What danger can be
> For us, the poor, the poor women of Canterbury ?
>   What tribulation
> With which we are not already familiar ?"
>
> (p. 11)

The tenor of their discourse in different from other characters. Their fears and apprehensions do not excite them. They are utterly passive. The state of omniscience robs their life of interest. They simply 'wait.' The term 'wait' is emphasised by its frequent repetition in their first song. They are to 'wait and witness.' like the audience. The audience share with them their fears, and their knowledge. The imagery of the chorus women is part of the larger pattern of the play's imagery. It intensifies the rhythm — internal structural rhythm of the drama. They sing of 'disastrous summer,' 'decaying October,' 'barren orchards,' 'ruinous spring' and 'happy December.' In the song before the entrance of Thomas on the stage, they sing of 'ill wind,' 'evil time,' 'bitter' and 'grey' sky foretelling the imminent danger. The paradigm of phrases that describe their lives convey the monotony and insignificance of life on this earth which is a basic feature of Eliot's ideology. The song moves at a slow leisurely pace :

> ... Yet we have gone of living
> Living and partly living.
> Sometimes the corn has failed us,
> Sometimes the harvest is good,
> One year is a year of rain
> Another a year of dryness
> One year the apples are abundant,
> Another year the plums are lacking
> Yet we have gone on living
> Living and partly living.
>
> (p. 15)

Boredom and meaninglessness of life are brought into foreground.

The monotony breaks into panic when the murder is executed. The panic and the hysteria of their song at that time foreground the magnitude of such crimes. Their illocutions persuade the audience to realize the thorough corruption in the universe. Their songs and dialogues and their language are the illocutionary acts of the playwright also as he directs, through them, the response of his audience in the direction he wants to. He makes the audience sympathize with the chorus and adore the martyr. The last choric song of thanks and praise wins reverence for the Archbishop as well as sympathy for the chorus who feel guilt and reproach themselves.

Eliot did not trust this device for shaping audience response and gave it up in the subsequent plays. *The Family Reunion* has only semi-chorus in the form of the aunts and uncles of the family. Eliot felt that the voice of collectively did not go with the contemporary sensibility and the jazz era. Though in rendering religious history in 'Murder in the Cathedral' it is used quite effectively.

THE FAMILY REUNION

Harry — the protagonist of the play — like Eliot, feels the problem of insufficient resources of language. He is suffering from a mysterious agony. He himself is only vaguely aware of the nature of his sufferings. He finds it difficult to put his experience into words. The mystery cannot be reduced to words. Harry feels that he cannot make other people understand his state of mind :

> Harry : But how can I explain, how can I explain to you ?
> You will understand less after I have explained it.
> All that I could hope to make you understand
> Is only events : not what has happened
> And people to whom nothing has ever happened
> Cannot understand the unimportance of events
> (p. 65)

The distinction that Harry makes between 'events' and 'what has happened' is a device to reveal the uniqueness of his experience. He withdraws part of the depth from the signifier 'event' and attaches and extra-significance to the word 'happen.' These subtleties of the usage of linguistic resources are the tools with which a playwright can hope to make his characters express themselves. Harry feels that his experience is entirely different from any experience of other people. The is arrogant enough to tell the members of his family that they are incapable of understanding him. He is baffled by a twofold gap — the gap between what he feels and what he explains and the gulf between what he explains and what others understand. The expression in terms of language does not match either with the speakers' real feeling or with the understanding of the listeners. The quality of the experience, the inadequacy of language resources and the level of understanding of the listeners are equally responsible for the two-fold gap.

As the drama proceeds we find, ironically, that Harry proves to be wrong in both of his hypotheses. Gradually, bit by bit, Harry unfolds his disturbed psyche. The experience of Harry and the understanding of his listeners remain the same. Linguistic repetitions and variations are exploited to convey the truth :

Harry : How can you sit in this blaze of light for all
the world to *look* at ?
If you knew how you *looked* when I *saw* you
through the window
Do you like to be *stared* by eyes through a window ?
Look there, *look* there; do you *see* them ?
No, No, not there, *look* there !
Can't you *see* them ? You don't *see* them, but
I *see* them
And they *see* me. This is the first time that
I have *seen* them.
....
The *eyes* stared at me, and corrupted that song
Behind the palm trees in the Grand Hotel
They were always there. But I didnot see them.

(p. 63)

The abundance of verbs of visual perception — look, see stare — convey a feeling that Harry's experience is concerned with 'seeing' something rare. He has gone through some extraordinary experience and has seen something that no one usually does. Harry is convinced of the uniqueness of his experience which increases his isolation. The sense of isolation results in a reflective tone. The tone of his dialogues moves inwards. He is reaching in the interior direction. That is part of the reason why he fails to communicate with the exterior world. His dialogues take the tone of soliloquies. He is obsessed with his spiritual tangle. He has not honestly begun to feel the need for communication.

To communicate the subtleties of his feelings Harry needs an individual use of language. His idiolect makes use of the terms 'events' and 'happen' in a unique way. He also makes a subtle distinction between 'sleep' and 'waking' — two states of mind as well as body.

Harry : You have gone through life in sleep
Never woken to the nightmare. I tell you life would be
unendurable
If you were wide awake.

(p. 65)

Harry has 'woken to the nightmare'. Life has changed its meaning for Harry. He has penetrated the spiritual reality. After the drowning of his wife in the mid-Atlantic Harry found himself awake, as if with a jolt. The term 'waking' has been made flexible to include within its premises a sense of sudden revelation. The other item in the pair, the term 'sleeping,' too is stretched until it includes spiritual lethargy in its territory. The signifier 'wide' reveals the acuteness of Harry's experience as well as the strain involved in keeping one's soul agile. The bewilderment of Harry's psyche leads to these specific meanings.

> Harry : You do not know
> The noxious smell untraceable in the drains
> Inaccessible to the plumbers, that has its hour of the
> night; you do not know
> The unspoken voice of sorrow in the ancient
> bedroom.
>
> (p.66)
>
> At three O'Clock in the morning. I am not speaking
> Of my own experience, but trying to give you
> Comparisons in a more familiar medium.
> I am the old house
> With the noxious smell and the sorrow before morning
> In which all past is present, all degradation
> Is unredeemable. As for what happens -
> Of the past you can only see what is past
> Not what is always present. That is what matters

Harry has begun to communicate 'in a more familiar medium.' The series of negatives — untraceable, inaccessible, unspoken — emphasize the inexpressible aspect of his experience. But since Harry is now prepared to speak in a familiar medium he begins the process of communication. The comparisons are of sensuous nature as the experience is acutely felt by Harry though it is not exactly sensuous. But the spiritual realities are by nature vague and abstract that cannot be defined sharply. Attempts to define the spiritual experience give us comparisons in terms of sense imagery. Harry, possibly, feels that other people can understand it in that way only. Agatha, Harry's aunt, understands his difficulty. She encourages him to continue talking in his 'own language.' Harry's language is highly metaphoric :

Harry : The sudden solitude in a crowded desert
In a thick smock, many creatures moving
Without direction, for no direction
Leads any where but round and round in that vapour
Without purpose, and without principle if conduct
In flickering intervals of light and darkness
The partial anesthesia of suffering without feeling
And partial observation of one's own automatism
While the slow stain sinks deeper through the skin
Tainting the flesh and discolouring the bone -
That is what matters, but it is unspeakable
Untranslatable : I talk in general terms
Because the particular has no language. One
thinks to escape
By violence, but one is still alone
In a overcrowded desert, jostled by ghosts
It was only reversing the senseless direction
For a momentary rest on the burning wheel
That cloudless nights in the mid Atlantic
When I pushed her over.

(p. 67)

Harry vacillates between 'general' and 'particular' and concludes that both are one. His sense of evil in the universe and his individual sense of sin both are rooted in a general sense of evil that human beings inherit — a basic tenet of Christianity. Harry's vision of the nightmare reality is expressed in an escalation of poetry to the climax and crisis of his blunt confession in plain prose. Eliot shocks us out of our complacency. The fact as well as the presentation are combined to reinforce the shock. The shifting of medium from poetry to prose is arresting.

The spiritual experience is repeatedly conveyed through images of the body. The images of skin, flesh, bone are put together to convey the sense of thorough physical corruption that results from spiritual bankruptcy. The anguish of Harry's soul is dramatized in the form of a richly connotative language. To enact the drama and reveal the truth in all its perspectives a series of images take on the roles of different characters — creatures moving in a thick smoke, round and round in the vapour; light and darkness flickering; the slow stain sinking deeper through the body; ghosts jostling the crowd; the burning wheel. Agatha — Harry's spiritual mentor -- follows the drama closely and seems to understand his dilemma.

> Harry : I think I see what you mean
> Dimly - as you once explained the sobbing in
> the chimney
> The evil in the dark closet, which they said was not
> there
> Which they explained away, but you explained them
> Or at least, made me cease to be afraid of them
> I will go and have my bath.
>
> (p. 68)

The last abrupt declaration shifts the focus of the drama from the inner to the outer world. The outer world realities could be expressed in prose. The inner drama needs poetry for its enactment because here words are the primary mode of action. Verbal events or speech acts are the major characters. They bring about the illocutionary and perlocutionary actions as desired by the speaker. Harry has been persuading others to believe that they are incapable of penetrating the mystery of his soul. Agatha successfully performs the speech act that convinces Harry that even he himself is only half aware of the mystery. Harry makes a distinction between 'explained away' and 'explained.' Agatha explained the mystery, she perceived the truth and put it across to Harry. She took the horror away from it and added a charm to the mystery. Whereas other people dismissed the mystery by explaining it away, by finding reason or logic in it. The context puts additional weight on the term 'explained.' The context overloads the simple terms with immense riches of meaning. To reverse the logic, the way words are used reveals the actual significance of the whole context. This pair of words makes a distinction between the two groups that the characters in the play are distributed into — the spiritually aware and the spiritually unaware characters. Agatha and Mary, along with Harry, are the awakened souls. Agatha and Mary perform significant verbal events to bring Harry round to the solution of spiritual mystery.

The verbal duets between Harry and Mary prove crucial to lead Harry towards a discovery of meaning in the presence of the agents from the world beyond. The lyrical dialogues between them elevate the drama to the spiritual plane. The language is accordingly highly poetic and symbolic :

Harry : I have spent many years in useless travel :
Your have stayed in England, yet you seem
Like someone who comes from a very long distance,
Or the distant waterfall in the forest,
Inaccessible, half-heard.
And I hear your voice as in the silence
Between tow storms, one hears the moderate usual noises
In the grass and leaves, of life persisting,
Which ordinarily pass unnoticed.
Perhaps you are right, though I donot know
How you should know it. Is the cold spring
Is the spring not an evil time, that excites us with lying voices ?

Mary : The cold spring now is the time
For the ache in the moving root
The agony in the dark
The slow flow throbbing the trunk
The pain of the breaking bud
These are the ones that suffer least :
The aconite under the snow
And the snow drop crying for a moment in the wood.

Harry : Spring is an issue of blood
A season of sacrifice
And the wail of the new full tide
Returning the ghosts of the dead
Those whom the winter drowned.
Do not the ghosts of the drowned
Return to land in the spring?
Do the dead want to return ?

Mary : Pain is the opposite of joy
But joy is a king of pain
I believe the moment of birth
Is when we have knowledge of death
I believe the season of birth
Is the season of sacrifice

For the tree and the beast, and the fish
Thrashing itself upstream :
And what of the terrified spirit
Compelled to be reborn
To rise toward the violent sun
Wet wings into the rain cloud
Here foot over the moon?

Harry : What have we been saying ? I think I was saying
That is seemed as if I had been always here
And you were someone who had come from a long
distance
Whether I know what I am saying, or why I say it,
That does not matter. You bring me news
Of a door that opens at the end of a corridor
Sunlight and singing, When I had felt sure
That every corridor only led to another,
Onto a blank wall; that I kept moving
Only so as not to stay still, Singing and light.
Stop !
What is that ? do you feel it

(pp. 81-82)

The communication between the two began at a high pitch and in the very first speech it was carried even higher to a dream like quality. While talking of 'Spring' they reveal the characteristic attitude of Eliot's character as discussed in the first play. They also play with pairs of words like pain/joy, life/death, light/dark. The lyrical tone exalts the communication to a spiritual level from where they soon come down, Harry asking what they have been saying.

Such poetic or lyrical dialogues are given up, in the subsequent plays, in favour of more realistic, conversational dialogues. After the spiritual communion Harry feels for the first time, a flicker of hope in his relationship with Mary. The images of door, corridor and sunlight and singling convey his sense of discovering a meaning and joy in life. But the moments of such joy — hope in terms of human relationship — are bound to be transient in the world of Eliot who finds meaning and permanent only in terms of supernatural realities. The divine messengers break the mood abruptly. The mode of presentation again shifts to prose, but this time the use of prose relates to the reality from the world of the supernatural. Harry finds their presence disturbing but he knows that he has got to face them squarely. He cannot avoid them. Mary pretends not to observe them and this enrages Harry. He reproaches Mary for having 'dull senses' and regrets listening to her nonsense.

Downing — Harry's driver — companion — has also seen these spiritual beings. He inhabits the borderline between the awakened and unawakened characters. For Downing — a simple man who belongs to the lower strata of society — they are 'ghosts.' His language — vocabulary, syntax, tone — reveal his social context.

Downing : Unlikely, Sir, if I may say so
Much more likely to have been an accident
I mean, knowing her ladyship
I don't think she had the courage

Charles : Did she ever talk of suicide ?

Downing : Oh yes, she did, every now and again
But in my opinion, it's those that talk
That are the least likely. To my way of thinking
She only did it to frighten people
If you take my meaning - just for the effect

Charles : I understand, Downing. Was she in good spirits ?

Downing : Well, always about the same, Sir
What I mean is, always up and down
Down in the morning, and up in the evening
And then she used to get rather excited
And in a way irresponsible, Sir
If I may make so bold, Sir ..

(p. 71)

He speaks with the fluency of informal conversation. He uses a simple, straight forward language. He is bold to face and speak the truth. His language has touches of colloquial features. He is the only character in the play to show a conversational ease. His diction is simple. The invisible hosts of heaven are 'ghosts' for him. For Agatha they are 'specters.' She qualifies them with varying attributes in an attempt to define their nature. They are :

Admonitious
From the world around the corner
The wind's talk in the dry holy tree

The inclination of the moon
The attraction of the dark passage
The paw under the door.

The precise nature and function of these mysterious beings is revealed in her speeches. Harry too uses abstract terms to refer to these creatures. Different words for the same phenomenon are put in the mouths of different characters. The differences in vocabulary reveal the differing states of spiritual evolution and intellectual apprehension. The spiritually awakened, aristocratic characters use an elevated, poetic register of language. Downing, though showing an equal level of spiritual awareness, uses a colloquial register and tone of language — which gives the play a wider appeal. The elevation and popularization motives are worked up simultaneously by the use of different registers of language for different groups of characters. Still Eliot falls short of that ideal fusion of the two that Yeats achieved in the later phase of his career.

THE COCKTAIL PARTY

'Mr. Eliot has attempted here something very daring and will worth doing. He has taken the ordinary West End drawing room comedy convention — understatement, upper class accent and all — and used it as a vehicle for utterly series ideas', *Observer.*[5]

The play aims, obviously, at popularization. 'under-statement' takes the place of elevated language of verse register. But serious, religious connotations exist underneath the mask of comedy. Eliot explores various dramatic and linguistic devices to bridge the gap between his serious, religious philosophy and a direct appeal which he found necessary for the dramatic mode. He reproduces contemporary speech rhythms in the play's dialogues. The seemingly comic and trivial dialogues conceal suggestions of serious nature. The comic tenor has undertones of ironic significance. A tension is generated in the language by this pull in two directions. — one towards the play's surface meaning and another towards its deeper implications suggested here and there. In other words it is a tension between this world and that world or between what is make believe and what is real. Sir Henry Reilly expresses it in terms of the natural human world and the supernatural or transhuman world while talking of Celia's experience.

> But such experiences can only be hinted at
> In myths and images. To speak about it
> We talk of darkness, labyrinths, Minotaur terrors
> But that world does not take the place of this one.

The tension between elevation and popularization is quite apparent in the language. Eliot splits the register in two - a surface register and a deep register. The religious connotations are kept at the deep level and are only hinted at. The surface of the language is symbolic and suggestive. Sir Reilly feels a necessity of indirect, symbolic expression but becomes conscious when he uses such a language. Sir Henry is the chief guardian figure. He is like a director guiding the action of the play. He is assigning roles to his patients — stripping off their assumed selves and revealing their true beings to them. He is their spititual mentor-cum-psychiatrist. Religious connotations are kept in a subordinate position. His register of language elevates the play above mere drawing room comedy. His tenor of discourse is apparently formal. His speech acts succeed at a marvellous speed owing to this style of speech that is highly tactful and efficient. In his role of an unidentified guest at Edward's party he creates suspense about himself by his mysterious silence and negative answer to all the enquires. When invited for a conversation by Edward he persuades him to want his wife back.

> Unidentified guest: There is certainly no purpose in remaining in
> the dark
> Except long enough to clear from the mind
> The illusion of having ever been in the light.
> The fact that you can't give a reason for
> wanting her
> Is the best reason for believing that you want her.
>
> Edward : I want to see her again - here.
>
> Unidentified guest : You shall see her again - here.
>
> (p. 136)

His style is that of a diplomat. he suggests in the beginning that whatever Edward loses by his wife's leaving him is for his good and that feeling 'ludicrous' or 'humiliated' are not harmful for him. His arguments lead Edward to confess and state with force that he wants his wife back. His diplomatic style proved very efficient to bring about the desired perlocutionary effect. Later in the play he makes a short appearance before Lavinia returns back. During this visit his dialogues suggest even stronger religious connotations from the surface register.

Unidentified guest : You will change your mind, but you are not free.
Your moment of freedom was yesterday.
You made a decision. You set in motion.
Forces in your life and in the lives of others
Which cannot be reversed. That is one consideration.
And another is this : it is a serious matter
To bring someone back from the dead.

Edward : From the dead ?
That figure of speech is some what ... dramatic
As it was only yesterday that my wife left me.

Unidentified guest : Ah, but we die to each other daily.
What we know of other people
Is only our memory of the moments
During which we know them. And they have changed since then.
To pretend that they and we are the same
Is a useful and convenient social convention
Which must sometimes be broken. We must also remember
That at every meeting we are meeting a stranger

(pp. 156-57)

His illocutions leave no scope for failure. He speaks in a confident, determined tone that shows a complete control of the situation. His neatly argued, rational style leaves little room for resistance. The listener is bound to perform the perlocutionary acts.

Edward, the protagonist, behaves as if he were a puppet in the hands of forces like Sir Henry that are beyond his control. Unlike the self-willed protagonists of Yeats' plays Eliot's protagonist speaks an entirely different language.

I see that my life was determined long ago
And that the struggle to escape from it

Is only a make believe, a pretence
That what is, is not, or could be changed
The self that can say I want this - or want that -
The self that wills - he is a feeble creature;
He has to come to terms in the end
With the obstinate, the tougher self; who doesnot speak
Who never talks, who cannot argue;
And who in some men may be the guardian -
But in men like me, the dull, the implacable,
The indomitable spirit of mediocrity.
The willing self can contrive the disaster
Of this unwilling partnership - but can only flourish
In submission to the rule of the stronger partner.

(p. 153)

The speech acts of Sir Henry have been instrumental in bringing about this self — revelating to Edward. Edward chooses to let the 'tougher,' 'unwilling' self prevail over the 'self that wills' — to merge his will with the will of the unknown forces as Thomas Archbishop did in *Murder in the Cathedral.* Yeats' protagonists spoke in a different manner and almost always chose to follow the 'self that wills' — Mary in *The Land of Heart's Desire,* Deirdre in *Deirdre,* Cuchulain in *At the Hawk's Well,* all chose the land of their heart's desire. They were not persuaded by the illocutions of other characters as do Eliot's protagonists. In Yeats the willing self is the tougher and obstinate self whereas in Eliot is is a 'feeble creature.' The difference in the qualifiers attached with the two types of selves amounts to a difference in their ideological base. The signifiers 'unwilling' and 'willing' are put to an individual use in Edward's idiolect — 'willing' means one that wills or has its own will and 'unwilling' means one that does not speak its will. Edward feels, just as Harry and the Archbishop do in earlier plays, a need to redefine certain concepts so that he can communicate his experience to others. It reveals their isolation from the group of other characters in the surrounding world.

Eliot deals with the concepts of 'real' and 'unreal' in each play. In this play we find that every character understands the two signifiers in its own individual manner and according to his/her own experience. Edward finds that his real self is 'the indomitable spirit of mediocrity'. He also discovers the futility of his attempts to escape into the 'Make-believe,' the unreal. His unreal self is 'the self that wills.' When Celia learns about Edward's reality she redefines her concepts of what is 'real' and what is 'unreal'.

> Can we only love
> Something created by our own imagination ?
> Are we all in fact unloving and unlovable ?
> Then one is alone, and if one is alone.
> Then lover and beloved are equally unreal
> And the dreamer is no more real than his dreams
>
> (p.188)

Her experience has revolutionized her thinking. It is revealed in her idiolect which defines various set concepts in its individual manner. She finds her 'vision' to be an 'illusion' and, therefore, everything on this side or existence seems to be 'unreal' to her. She assigns special meaning to some other ideas.

> No ... it is n't that I want to be alone
> But that everyone's alone - or so it seems to me.
> They make noises, and think they are talking to each other
> They make faces, and think they understand each other
> And I am sure that they don't. Is that a delusion ?
>
> (p. 156)

Celia learns the meaning of 'delusion' in terms of her own experience. Her experience has been an intensely shattering one. What seemed 'talking' earlier becomes 'making noise' for her and what was 'understanding' becomes 'making faces.' She attaches a wider range of meaning with the terms talking and understanding as well as with making noise and making faces. She reshuffles the relationships between various signifiers and signifieds in terms of her own experience. Her isolation from the surrounding world reaches deeper than the isolation of Edward as she is a visionary who finds herself disillusioned. While talking to Sir Henry her language becomes highly abstract and her tone suggests a moment towards her innerself. She uses a spiritual and philosophical register.

> Celia : Well, my bringing up was pretty conventional -
> I had always been taught to disbelieve in sin,
> Oh, I don't mean that it was ever mentioned !
> But anything wrong, from our point of view,

Was either bad form, or was psychological.
And bad form always led to disaster
Because the people one knew disapproved of it.
I don't worry much about form, myself -
But when everything is bad form, or mental kinks,
You either become bad form, and cease to care,
Or else, if you care, you must be kinky. (p. 187)

Celia seems to have gone very far in the interior of her mind. She becomes vague about her feelings and in her language. This is the only method by which she can relate to her experience.

Peter refers to his experience in terms of reals and unreal while talking to Edward.

I have been telling you of something real
My first experience of reality

Peter speaks about his relationship with Celia. After discovering the change in Celia he too redefined his concept of reality.

What is the reality
Of experience between two unreal people ?

Celia and Peter both discover the unreality of what they thought real experiences. Eliot did not believe, at this stage, in the reality of this world and the people and relationships on this side of the grave. His ideology is reflected in the language of his characters.

The language of the play is "the transparent poetry for which he had been working."[6] The element of comedy is blended with the language as the comedy is 'alive as a succession of diverting incidents ... it is alive in the conversational and debating thrusts of the dialogue. It is alive in the metrics of the dialogue."[7] The language of Julia is representative of such live comedy. But the figure of Julia is much more significant than being a mere source of comedy.

Eliot's method of presentation is best reflected in the person of Julia. She represents the serious philosophy hidden behind the guise of modern frivolity. In her the drawing room world of modern London co-exists with the spiritual world of Eliot. She provides most of the informal chatter at the parties. Yet she is one of the guardian figures. She is Sir Henry's link between the two worlds. She puts on a very transparent mask of selfishness and frivolity over her extremely sincere concern for other people and their happiness. She is like a person who plays the joker in order that other people may laugh. Her sincerity of concern for other people is revealed when she visits Sri Henry.

> We must take the risk.
> All we could do was to give them the chance.
> And now, when they are stripped naked to their souls
> And can choose, whether to put on proper costumes.
> Or huddle quickly into new disguise. They have,
> For the first time, some were to start from.
>
> (p. 193)

She can communicate very smoothly in the world of Sir Henry as well as in the world represented by Lavinia-Edward, Celia-Peter. Her mask of frivolity is only a mask as is the comedy of the play. The play is not a comedy in the true sense. Comic and light dialogues are only Eliot's devices that mask his religious philosophy. Eliot resorted to these devices in order to get popular appeal for his plays and inject his ideology into the minds of his audience. His intention was not mere entertainment but to bring about a spiritual awakening in the society. The dialogue of the play work on two planes. On the surface they entertain and when we dig a bit deeper they provide food for the mind.

THE CONFIDENTIAL CLERK

> Sir Claude: But when I am alone, and look at one thing long though
> I sometimes have that sense of identification
> With the maker of which I spoke - an agonising ecstasy
> Which makes life bearable. It's all I have
> I suppose it takes the place of religion :
> Just as my wife's investigations
> Into what she calls the life of the spirit
> Are a kind of substitute for religion
> I dare say, truly religious people
> I have never known any - can find some unity
> Then there are also the men of genius.
> There are others - it seems to me, who have at best to live

In two worlds - each a kind of make-believe.
That's you and me ...
(p. 238)

Sir Claude's definition of 'real' and 'make believe' is another version of the two signifiers that form the crucial basis of Eliot's idiolect. 'Real' signifies a sense of identification of unification with the maker - a unity of 'maker' and the 'made.' Sir Claude suggests another realm of reality that men of genius too are capable of achieving, apart from truly religious people. The term 'make believe' is reserved for all mediocre intellects. Lack of unity makes both the worlds unreal for Sir Claude.

Mr. Colby Simpkins too is seen discovering the meaning of what is real and what is unreal during his conversation with Lucasta. The language of the dialogue between Colby and Lucasta shows an ascending pattern. Their speeches show a progression from argumentative, intellectual style to almost lyrical speech rhythm. In the beginning they are seen discussing and debating.

Lucasta : What about taking me to a concert ?

Colby : Only the other day, I invited you ...

Lucasta : To go to see that American Musical ?

Colby : Well, I'd heard you say you wanted to see it.

Lucasta : But not with you !

Colby : You made that very clear
But why no with me ?

Lucasta : Because you don't like them -
American Musical. Do you think it is my compliment
That is just being .... patronising. But if you invite me
To something you like - that is a compliment.
It shows you want to educate me

Colby : But I didn't know
That you wanted to be educated

Lucasta : Neither did I
But I wanted you to want to educate me
And now I'm beginning to believe that I want it.

Colby : Well, I'm going to invite you to the next concert.

Lucasta : The next that you want to go to yourself.

(pp. 242-43)

Their style of speech is simple, conversational without metrical regularity. They are beginning to make attempts at understanding each other. As they proceed their speeches becomes more rhythmic and poetic.

Colby : I'm being very serious
Want I mean is, my garden is no less unreal to me
Than the world outside it. It you have two lives
Which have nothing whatever to do with each other
Well, they're both unreal. But for Eggerson
His garden is a part of one single world.

Lucasta : But what do you want ?

Colby : Not to be alone there.
If I were religious. God would walk in my garden
And that would make the world outside it real
And acceptable, I think

Lucasta : You sound awfully religious
Is there no other ways of making it real to you ?

Colby : It is simply the fact of being alone there
That makes it unreal.

Lucasta : Can no one else enter ?

Colby : It can't be done by issuing invitations :
They would just have to come. And I should not see
them coming

I should not hear the opening of the gate.
They would simple ... be there suddenly,
Unexpectedly. Walking down an alley
I should become aware of some one walking with me
That's the only way I can thing of putting it.

Lucasta : How afraid one is ... of being hurt !

Colby : It's not the hurting that one would mind
But the sense of desolation afterwards.

Lucasta : I know what you mean. Then the flowers would fade
And the music would stop. And the walls would be broken
And you would find yourself in a devastated area -
A bomb site ... willow herb ... a dirty public square.
(pp. 245-46)

What Colby signifies by unreal is the same version of Sir Claude's story. Fragmented selves are not real for Colby. Only unity of being is real. Colby thinks that 'reality' can be achieved in terms of human relationship as well. That is a significant digression in Eliot's ideology. Though their attempts to reach reality are thwarted and ultimately checked. Eliot at least expressed a possibility of finding reality in this very life. The concept of reality has undergone a major change in Eliot's idiolect as will be proved in the next play.

Lucasta and Colby are growing in understanding of each other. Their conversation takes on emotional under-tones. Unlike the images of door, alley, and rose garden in *The Family Reunion* the register of this play's language is more modern and urban. They use images such as 'bomb site' and 'public square.' The drama becomes intensified as their conversation becomes more imaginative. At the climax it picks up momentum. Their speech rhythm becomes almost lyrical.

Colby : There's no end to understanding a person
All one can do is to understand them better
To keep up with them; so that as the other changes
You can understand the change as soon as it happens,
Though you couldn't have predicted it.

Lucasta : I think I'm changing
I've changed quite a lot in the last two hours

Colby : And I think I'm changing too. But perhaps what
We call change...

Lucasta : Is understanding better what one really is.
And the reason why that comes about, perhaps ...

Colby : Is beginning to understand another person.

Lucasta : Oh Colby, now that we begin to understand,
I'd like you to know a little more about me.

When the conversation began they were making attempts, by arguing, to understand each other. The style was rational and has remained so throughout as the excessive use of the term understand bears out. But their understanding has grown up during the dialogue. Now they are in harmony with each other's ideas. They do not need to argue. Their speeches are complementary. A perfect rapport has been established between them. Both of them have successfully performed their illocutionary acts and now they begin to understand each other. The style of language remains intellectual or rational but the rhythms of speech have changed from argumentative to lyrical. The ideas and images are simple and a testimony of Eliot's shift in dramatic goals. Eliot is aiming at a larger audience.

Colby's tenor of discourse is very formal with Sir Claude as is their relationship. He uses a very polite language as he thinks of him 'rather as a patron than a father.'

> Colby : May I ask
> With this passion for ... ceramics, how did it happen
> That you never made it your profession ?

Sir Claude used the term 'potter' without any hesitation. But Colby is obviously too formal to use the colloquial alternative for the term 'ceramics.' He is not able to squeeze the distance created over the years of separation between them. But the same Colby does not mind using a highly colloquial register of language when in a different environment and with different people.

With Lucasta and B. Kagan, Colby is more open and frank. The three of them are quite informal in their tenor. Their idiom is colloquial and words with strong emotional undertones are not shunned out which is a rare occasion in Eliot's world.

> Kagon : Marriage is a gamble. But I'm a born gambler
> And I've put my shirt ... no, not quite the right
> expression
> Lucasta's the most exciting speculation
> I've ever thought of investing in.
> Colby's more cautious. You know, Colby,
> You and I ought to be in business together.
> I'm a good guesser. But I sometimes guess wrong
> I make decisions on the spur of the moment,

	But you'd never take a leap in the dark; You'd keep me on the rails
Colby :	That's just nonsense You only pretend that you're a gambler You've got as level a head as anyone And you never get involved in anything risky You like to pretend to other people That you're a gambler. I don't believe you ever gamble
Kaghan :	Well, there's something in that. You know, Lucasta, Colby is a good judge of character.
Lucasta :	You'd need to be a better judge of character Yourself, before you said that of Colby
Kaghan :	Oh, I'm a good judge.

(p. 252)

B. Kaghan's style is the most colloquial of all the three. He does not care to modify his statements that are flat generalization sometimes. Their conversation is in the informal, intimate style.

We find ourselves in an entirely different world when we enter the room where the crucial meeting about Colby's real parenthood takes place. The meeting is arranged with the seriousness of a ritual. It is carried out with high formality and extreme care. Sir Claude's style is circumlocutory, inclined towards formality in its tenor of discourse. Mrs. Guzzard was not received at the door and it is called 'domestic incompetence' by Sir Claude. Sir Claude asks Eggerson to preside over and conduct the proceedings. Eggerson formally announces the starting of the meeting giving it a solemnity that concerns the 'problem of paternity.' The language and style of the meeting take the immediate context of Colby's parenthood to general level. The spiritual quest of an individual that is suggested by the generalization is kept carefully hidden. After a series of revelations during the meeting very one emerges a different person. Everyone seem to understand better his own self as well as the other people, even the dead ones. The revelations lead to redefine some of the concepts in terms of new insight

Sir Clude : What he wanted to transmit to me
Was that idea, that inspiration
Which to him was life. To me, it was a burden
You can't communicate an inspiration,
Like that, by force of will. He was a great financier
And I am merely a successful one.
I might have been truer to my father's inspiration
If I had done what I wanted to do.

(p. 266)

Sir Claude, now, understands the finer distinction between the two terms 'great' and 'successful'. Before the discovery of the truth about inspiration the two signifiers signified the same thing. The concept of inspiration too is redefined. Growth of understanding leads to a refinement of language and this refinement, in turn, leads to a still better understanding of one's own self and the other people.

THE ELDER STATESMAN

Eliot has come a long way from religious drama in *Murder in the Cathedral* to the tragic comedy of *The Family Reunion.* The mood alters with the West End comedy *The Cocktail Party* and from there onwards to the farcial comedy — *The Confidential Clark,* leading finally to the romantic comedy *The Elder Statesmen.* The gradual change in his dramatic form reflects his increasing desire to reach larger and larger segments of society. To integrate his dramatic goals with his poetic goals Eliot happened to make his poetry less and less conspicuous or obtrusive. As a consequence his language shows a continuous movement towards transparency and thinness. The image of weather, birds and beasts, and heavily philosophical speeches and spiritual terminology of the earlier plays like *Murder in the Cathedral* and *The Family Reunion* are completely abandoned in the last plays. The three-dimensional images like rose garden, door and sensuous images of the first two plays are replaced by comparatively flat analogies from the everyday world of material progress.

Lord Claverton : A fear of the vacuum, and no desire to fill it.
It's just like sitting in an empty waiting room
In a railway station on a branch line,

After the last train, after all the other passengers
Have left, and the booking office is closed
And the porters have gone.

(p. 302)

The register of language is modernised — a process that began with the last play *The Confidential Clerk.*

The shift in the dramatic form and the linguistic form is accompanied by, or is a consequence of, change in Eliot's ideology. Eliot's concepts of divine and human, real and make-believe have gone through a significant transformation. Eliot moves progressively towards bringing the two planes of existence close to each other. From a complete rejection of human love in *The Family Reunion* Eliot comes to discover, in *The Elder Statesman,* that human love can lead to divine love, thus, uniting and complementing the human and superhuman planes.

Monica : Oh Father, I've always loved you
But I love you more since I have come to know you
Here at Badgley Court. And I love you the more
Because I love Charles.

Lord Clavertion : Yes, my dear,
Your love is for the real Charles, not a make believe
As was your love for me.

Monica : But not now, father !
It's the real you I love — the man you are.
Not the man I thought you were.

Lord Claverton : And Michael
I love him, even for rejecting me
For the me he rejected, I reject also.
I've been freed from the self that pretends to be
someone
And in becoming none, I begin to live.

(pp. 353-54)

The concept of fatherhood belongs to both the planes of existence — human and divine. The signifier 'real' signifies reality on both the planes. Monica reaches divine love via human love. Lord Claverton leaves the make-believe for the real. The concepts of real and make believe, human and spiritual are integrated into a single pattern.

The concepts of true or real self and mask of role playing have been recurring motifs in Eliot's plays. The chorus women in *The Family Reunion* felt that they were like unwilling actors who played their assigned roles. The semi-chorus figures, uncles and aunts of Harry too felt themselves to be like the actors who had rehearsed wrong parts. Edward and Lavinia in *The Cocktail Party* were stripped naked to their souls, by the guardian figure Sir Henry. Before the revelation they went on playing roles assigned to them by each other. B. Kaghan, Lucasta, Sir Claude and Lady Elizabeth all discover their true selves only at the end in *The Confidential Clerk.* Lord Claverton assumes the mask of an elder statesman in the present play. He too discovers his true being only at the end of the drama which coincides with the end of his life. He put on the mask which he took to be the real self for the whole life. Gomez calls it a failure.

> Gomez : The worst kind of failure, in my opinion,
> Is the man who has to keep on pretending to himself
> That he's a success - the man who in the morning
> Has to make up his face before he looks in the mirror.
>
> (p. 312)

The signifier 'failure' signifies a different dimension of meaning in Gomez's idiolect. Gomez is the part of Lord Claverton's past that he would rather forget. He reminds him of his failure. Mrs. Carghill, another ghost from his past, too knows the real self of Lord Claverton that he has hidden behind the mask. She admires his ability to play any role. 'whatever part you've played. I must say you've always looked it.' The register of stage acting has occurred in each of his plays but this last play brings it into focus. Role playing becomes the dominant theme of the play and dropping of the costumes is the central action. The process of discovery of one's true self makes the drama. A series of speech-acts from the characters of dubious nature, like Gomez and Mrs. Carghill, hasten the revelations :

Mrs. Carghill : ....
At bottom, I believe you're still the same silly
Richard
You always were. You wanted to pose
As a man of the world. And now you're posing
As What ? I presume, as an elder statesman
And the difference between being an elder
statesman
And posing successfully as an elder statesman
In practically negligible. And you look the part.
Whatever part you've played, I must say
You've always looked it.

Lord Claverton : I've no longer any part to play, Maisie.

Mrs. Cargill : There will always be some sort of part for you
Right to the end. You'll still be playing a part
In your obituary, whoever writes it.

(p. 324)

After a number of confrontations with Michael, Gomez and Mrs. Carghill, Lord Claverton realises his mistake. The realization descends upon Lord Claverton and he confesses the truth to Monica and Charles.

Lord Claverton : I've spent my life trying to forget myself
In trying to identify myself with the part
I had chosen to play. And the longer we pretend
The harder it becomes to drop the pretence
Walk off the stage, change into our own clothes
And speak as ourselves. So I'd become an idol
To Monica. She worshipped the part I played :
How could I be sure that she would love the
actor
If she saw him off the stage, without his
costumes and make up
And without his stage words.

(pp. 340-41)

The images of stage, costume, and actor are emphasized with an intensity that betrays some hidden designs, besides displaying the real drama : Eliot perhaps had calculated that this idiom would amuse his audiences; or he might himself have felt a necessity to drop a certain mask that he put on during his career as a playwright.

The final conversation between Charles and Monica, like the dialogue between Colby and Lucasta in *The Confidential Clerk*, reveals a progression towards increased lyricism that accompanies that growth of understanding between the two :

> Monica : Charles, though we've been alone to-day
> Only a few minutes, I've felt all the time ...
>
> Charles : I know what you're going to say !
> We were alone together, in some mysterious fashion,
> Even with Michael, and despite those people,
> Because somehow we'd begun to belong together,
> And that awareness ...
>
> Monica : Was a shield protecting both of us ...
>
> Charles : So that now we are conscious of a new person
> Who is you and me together.
>
> (pp. 354-55)

Their speeches are left incomplete and are completed by each other. The communication proceeds with a lyrical fluency. The speaker changes but the ideas continue, on and on, as if it were a single speech. It is a perfect speech act. A perfect harmony and oneness exists between the two Eliot, who did not show the unification of Lucasta and Colby in *The Confidential Clerk*, lets the two lovers at large in this play. They are not prohibited from finding happiness in terms of each other. The divine figure, that each of the earlier protagonists pursued, does exist in this play as well and is pursued in the form of Monica's father but this time without leaving the human companion.

> behind : Monica declares,
> We will go to him together.

Eliot, who found rievalry in the relationship between the human and the superhuman in *The Family Reunion*, comes to discover a sense of harmony between the two. It is exhibited in the mood of the play which is enveloped in peace and serenity.

REFERENCES :

Note: All the quotations from the plays refer to the *Collected Plays* of T.S. Eliot.

1. T.S. Eliot, 'Poetry and Drama'. *On Poetry and Poets*, p. 79.
2. Katharine Worth, 'Eliot and the Living Theatre,' *Eliot in Perspective,* ed. Graham Martin, p. 148.
3. See R.S. Pathak, ed., *New Directions in Eliot Studies,* pp. 19-30.
4. See E. Martin Brown, *The Making of T.S. Eliot's Plays*, p. 42.
5. See *The Cocktail Party,* back cover.
6. Herbert Howarth, *Notes on Some Figures behind T.S. Eliot,* p. 331.
7. *Ibid.*, p. 330.

Chapter Five

Achievement

The exploration of the linguistic dimension of their plays through categories opened up by modern language studies helps us to see especially how the text works as discourse. The ideological intent of Yeats and Eliot, which is to elevate and popularize poetic drama, and the value-emphasis in the conceptual content of their plays is borne out by the selection. combination and repetition of language features, so as to draw attention to the nature of the experiment the two dramatists were conducting.

Yeats and Eliot heralded the revival of poetic drama with the intention to reform the deterioration in public taste that various popular forms of theatre were bringing about. Their aims were not only literary or aesthetic, but also socio-cultural and religious. Yeats evolved a total art of theatre and experimental with various dramatic techniques. He was aiming at reawakening heroic passions dormant in racial memory which would further the cause of Ireland's struggle for its freedom. He intended to evolve a form of drama that would demand a complete involvement — intellectual, emotional, imaginative — on the part of the audience. Eliot too intended to elevate as well as popularize poetic drama. He wanted to propagate his religious world view and awaken the audience to the spiritual reality visible only 'out of the corner of the eye.'

Their respective aims and ideologies took definite shapes at various levels of language — lexical, syntactic, semantic and interactive. Their practices ad playwrights give us ample evidence that a close correspondence existed between variations or shifts in emphasis in their aims and their linguistic techniques. The ideological antagonism between the two playwrights is fully borne out by their language.

Yeats sets a peasant dialect against elevated heroic register in the first phase of his playwriting. Gradually the directness of colloquial idiom begins to play a major role leaving small space for heroic dialogues on the stage. For a few plays in the middle of his career Yeats combined the registers of prose and poetry. But he did not retain prose in the later plays. We find further, that at the climax of his career he wrote dance plays after the Noh techniques. Lyrics, dance and highly stylized action are the hallmarks of these plays. Lyrical and dramatic are integrated in them.[1] The element of songs, that played a secondary role in the early plays becomes blended with the action of the dance-drama. Songs and dance become the primary mode of exposition of dance drama. They enact the central emotion in certain of his plays, apart from the plays for dancers.

In the later phase Yeats shaped his rhythms following the rhythms of folk balla ds. Ballad rhythms strike a harmonious chord with his own romantic bent of mind as well as with the memories of his audience which are attached to folk music. Yeats' blending of ballad rhythms in his drama marks a progress towards the achievement of his basic intention of elevation- popularization.[2]

Yeats' plays display 'an absolute mastery of language,' 'structural fineness,'[3] and cohesion of different arts. The poetry of Yeats' plays is the poetry of cohesion of varied elements of drama and language into a single whole. His achievement as a verse playwright parallels his political, cultural and literary ponderings.

T.S. Eliot's judgment of W.B. Yeats' achievement as a verse playwright is worth quoting here.[5]

> "... to me Yeats is a type of lyrical dramatist ... Yeats did not quite invent a new metre, but the blank verse of his later plays shows a great advance towards one; and what is most astonishing is the virtual abandonment of blank verse metre in *Purgatory*. One device used with great success in some of the later plays is the lyrical choral interlude. Yet another, and

> important cause of improvement is the gradual purging out of poetical ornament. This perhaps is the most painful part of the labour, of the modern poet who tries to write a plays in verse, so far as the versification goes. The course of improvement is towards a greater and greater starkness."

Eliot noticed the gradual starkness of Yeats' versification. But Yeats was simultaneously moving towards enrichment of his language through symbolism, mysticism and stylization. He has creatively explored the various fields, modes and tenors of discourse; performed effective speech-acts while exploring the various levels of the language dimension. By a polarization of language and style between heroic and mundane, elevated and colloquial he has foregrounded his evaluation of experience which is diametrically opposed with Elite's understanding of life is this universe. Yeats' complex mysticism and practices in the occult enriched the symbolism of his language and stylized the drama. He did not prescribe to Eliot's doctrine of 'purging out of poetical ornament' in the sense Eliot himself did. On the contrary Yeats did not shun the element of artifice in his drama and its language which is best evidenced by the practice of his dance plays.

Eliot himself has gradually purged out 'the poetical ornament' of his own plays. The densely poetic and symbol laden register of poetry that Eliot used in *The Murder in the Cathedral* is brought closer to the drawing room register of the urban elite in the next play *The Family Reunion.* In *The Family Reunion* Eliot seems to fuse successfully the elevated language of poetry and the dramatic intensity of action which is an ideal for poetic drama. Dialogues are imitative of actual conversational rhythms. Afterwards Eliot's drama reveals a linear progression towards a greater and greater simplification of language which is motivated by his desire to popularize poetic drama.

Eliot's move towards 'transparency' in his language in now rapid. The plays are marked by a 'plainness,' to use Yeats' word, or 'directness' as Eliot call it :

> "In my youth, I think that Dante's astonishing economy and directness of language, his arrow that goes unerringly to the centre of the target -

> Provided for me a wholesome corrective to the extravagances of Elizabethan, Jacobean and Caroline authors in whom I also delighted."[6]

The Cocktail Party owes its comic exuberance to its directness of language and conversational or debating thrusts of the dialogue. *The Confidential Clerk* shows the same tendency towards simplicity. The farcical element in it is accentuated by appropriate uses of language and style; by overdoing the formalities at the crucial meeting about Colby's parenthood, for example. The features that lead to its farcical nature also conceal the serious connotations behind the apparently insignificant details.

The last play *The Elder Statesman* follows the same pattern. It keeps its deeper meaning still closely guarded, by the romantic element in the language as well as in the drama. Eliot has completely abandoned the poeticisms of his earlier plays in favour of a conversational ease and informality that pervades the whole play.

Yeats and Eliot both show an inclination towards a blending of the actual and colloquial speech rhythms in the fabric of their drama. Though Eliot seems to overdo it. unlike Yeats who kept a balance between the elevated and colloquial registers and styles of his plays' language, Helen Gardner gives equal credit to both the playwrights for their inclusion of the 'colloquial' that left its mark on the following generations :

> "The most important and the greatest legacy that poets so different as Yeats, Pound, and Eliot left to their successors was not their theories about the nature of poetry, nor their always very partial adoption of the symbolist aesthetic, but their reinvigoration of the language of poetry by bringing it into relation with contemporary and colloquial speech."[7]

The contention of basic values between the two writers is borne out by their language and style at every level. Since Yeats believed and wanted to promote faith in the heroic indomicability of individual will his protagonists defeat the illocutionary forces applied upon them from different quarters. Eliot's characters, on the contrary, perform speech acts successfully directing the protagonist towards a merger of his will with the divine will. Eliot puts his faith in the merging of human will with the divine will.

The goal of popularization led Eliot to explore the possibilities of modern drawing room conversation of the urban elite as the language of his plays. Eliot enriched the empty chatter of the ordinary dialogue with ironic significance, to suggest more than levels of meaning. He reproduced the rhythms of actual conversation in the dialogues of his plays. The songs in his plays sometimes echoes the rhythms of popular jazz music.

Yeats' search for a larger audience led him to explore the poetic richness of country dialect for the dialogues of his plays and the rhythms of popular folk ballads for the songs. Yeats resorts to the traditional, the rural, as opposed to Eliot who routes the rhythms and style of his language towards the modern and urban.

Besides being modern Eliot is essentially rational in his approach. The tone of argumentation and a concentration of terms of mental perception in the dialogues of his plays are indications of his intellectual bent of mind. It leads to a riddling quality in his characters' speeches that account for the appeal of his plays to the upper class London society.

Yeats, quite differently, sought for words that ooze out passion. He put his faith in the intuitive response to life. He hated passionless reasoning. The passionate intensity leads to an irregular syntax which is held together by the force of passion only. This quality is consonant with his belief in the traditional and rural as Eliot's modernity is in harmony with his rationality. If Eliot's appeal was wider then Yeats' appeal must have been deeper.

Yeats juxtaposes different secular registers — the heroic and the peasant in the beginning of his career as a playwright. Eliot juxtaposes religious and mundane or spiritual and ordinary registers for his spiritually awakened and unawakened characters. Those who have glimpsed the supernatural reality and strive after religious truth speak an elevated register whereas those who are ignorant to supernatural existence are given a simple, everyday register of language. Eliot puts supernatural several steps ahead of the natural. Yeats, quite differently, makes them complementary. If Forgael of *The Shadowy Waters* yearns for some experience of supernatural intensity then the woman of the Sidhe in *The Only Jealousy of Emer* is also shown yearning for human passion. Because they are kept on an equal footing they do not speak entirely different registers of language.

Yeats, aiming at 'a profane perfection of manking,' considers this life superior to the abstract reality that the supernatural world is. His belief in this life results in his belief in conflict, tension, vigour or energy that are the components of life. His poetry and drama emerge from 'the rag and bone shop of heart.' He adhered to his faith in life and exalted its virtues. Eliot on the other hand places his belief in the religious, supernatural plane of existence that demands austerity in life. He belittles the virtues of life on this side of the grave. His language makes the chaos of an individual's inner self that Yeats' language reveals so beautifully, in *On Baile's Strand* for example. Eliot portrays the inner conflict of the Archbishop's self in *Murder in the Cathedral* but, there too, in theory, he shuns action. He makes the Archbishop conclude that he is not to 'act.' Action, the root of life as well as the root of poetry and drama is distrusted. Emotions are equally suspected. This ideological antagonism pervades every aspect of the creation of Yeats and Eliot. It permeats their language, rhythm, technique etc.

Eliot, in his efforts to elevate and popularize drama turns to simplification of language. The secular, modern language hides ironic undertones that suggest the higher plane of existence. The facade of contemporaneity, that is supposed to win popularity for his drama conceals deeper, religious meanings. Yeats on the other hand turns to the roots of poetry and drama. He reproduces the traditional ballad rhythms and colloquial rhythms. He attempts to attain popularity without doing away with elevation. He juxtaposes and blends together the 'high' with 'low' styles of language at lexical, phonological and discoursal levels and, therefore, attains greater success in terms of this basic intention.

REFERENCE :

1. G.S Fraser, *The Modern Writer and His World*, p. 54.

   Fraser felt differently about Yeats' plays : "Here an absolute mastery of language, a speculative mind playing profoundly with symbols, a deep and real feeling for Irish tradition and its folk roots, somehow fail to compensate for a lack of that dramatic 'body' whcih we tend to look for in action and characters of a real play".

2. C.L. Wrenn, *Word and Symbol : Studies in English Language*, pp. 193-94. Wrenn felt that Yeats' "Interest in the genuine ballads of the people — as witnessed by his efforts late in life to recite verse in the traditional folk style of the oral ballad — probably helped Yeats to that blend of colloquial language and poetic thought and imagery which Mr. Eliot, like him, has been seeking."

3. Eenis Donoghue, *The Third Voice*, p. 248. D. Donoghue found "the structural fineness of Yeats' Noh plays — the measure of his superiority." For this reason he considers him "a better poete de theatre than Eliot or James Joyce."

4. James W. Flannery, *W.B. Yeats and the Idea of a Theatre*, pp. 312-13. "At his best Yeats was not merely a poet in the theater but a poetic dramatist who combined the arts of literature and the theatre so as to create effective and profoundly significant drama."

5. T.S. Eliot, Yeats', *On Poety and Poets*, p. 134.

6. T.S. Eliot, *To Criticise the Critic*, p. 22.

7. Helen Gardener, 'Present Discontents,' *Contemporary Criticism*, ed. V. Seturaman, p. 523.

Bibliography

PRIMARY SOURCES

BOOKS

Eliot, T.S. *After Strange Gods.* London : Faber and Faber, 1934.

--- *Collected Plays.* London : Faber and Faber, 1962.

--- *The Sacred Wood : Essays on Poetry and Criticism.* London : Mathuen and Co., 1967.

--- *On Poetry and Poets.* London : Faber and Faber, 1965.

--- *Selected Essays.* London : Faber and Faber, 1951.

Yeats, W.B. *Autoboigraphies.* London : Macmillian, 1956.

--- *Essays and Introductions.* London : Macmillan, 1961.

--- *Explorations.* London : Macmillan, 1962.

--- *Mythologies.* London : Macmillan, 1959.

--- *The Collected Plays.* London : Macmillan, 1952.

--- *The Collected Poems.* London : Macmillan, 1950.

--- Plays and Controversies. London : Macmillan, 1925.

ARTICLES IN PERIODICALS :

Eliot, T.S. "A Commentary." *The Criterion*, XI (April, 1932).

--- "A Commentary." *The Criterion*, XI (July, 1932).

--- "A Commentary." *The Criterion*, XII (Jan., 1933).

--- "A Commentary." *The Criterion*, XIII (April, 1933)

--- "Ulysses, Order and Myth." *The Dial,* LXXV (November, 1928).

--- "Indiscretions." *Times Literary Supplement,* (September 16-22, 1988).

SECONDARY SOURCES

BOOKS

Adams, Joseph. *Yeats and the Masks of Syntax.* London : The Macmillan Press Ltd., 1984.

Allen, J.P.B. & Corder, S.P.T. *The Edinburgh Course in Applied* Linguistics. 4 vols., London : Oxford University Press, 1975.

Alspack, Russel K., ed. *The Variorum Edition of the Plays of W.B. Yeats.* London : Macmillan, 1966.

Armstrong, W.A. Intro. *Classic Irish Drama.* W.B. Yeats. Middlesex : Penguin, 1964.

Bahri, U.S. *Papers in Language and Linguistics.* Vols. I-II, New Delhi : Bahri Publications P. Ltd., 1986.

Bate, W.I. *From Classics to Romantic : Premises of Taste in Eighteenth Century England.* Harward University Press, 1946.

Bazell, C.E., Cateford, J.C. Halliday M.A.S., Robins, R.H. eds. *In Memory of J.R. Firth.* London : Longman Group Limited, 1966.

Bentley, Eric. *The Dramatic Event.* London : Dennis Dobson, 1956.

--- The *Playwritht as Thinker.* New York : Reynal and Hitchcock, 1946.

Bieber, Margareta. *The History of the Greek and Roman Theatre.* Princeton, Princeton University Press, 1961.

Bloomfiefl, Leonard. *Language.* New Delhi : Motilal Banarsidas, 1935.

Boulton, Marjorie. *The Anatomy of Drama.* London : Routledge and Kegan Paul Ltd., 1960.

--- *The Anatomy of language.* New Delhi : Kalyani Publishers, 1959.

Brooks, Cleanth. *Tragic Themes in Western Literature.* New Haven : Yale University Press, 1955.

Brook, G.L. *English Dialects.* London : Andre Deutsch Ltd., 1963.

Braybrooks, Neville. *T.S. Eliot : A Symposium for his Seventieth Birthday.* London : Rupert Hart Davis, 1958.

Brennan, Anthony. *Shakespeare's Dramatic Structures.* London : Routledge, 1986.

Browne, E. Martin, *The Making of T.S. Eliot's Plays.* Cambridge : Cambridge University Press, 1955.

Chiari, Joseph. *T.S. Eliot : Poet and Dramatist.* London : Vision Press Limited, 1972.

Clark David R. *Twentieth Century Interpretation of Murder in the Cathedral.* New Jersey : Prentice Hall, 1971.

Cole, Toby, ed. *Play wrights on Play Writing.* London : Macgibban and Kee, 1960.

Coyle Martin, Garside Peter, Kelsall Malcolm and Peck John. *Encyclopaedia of Literature and Criticism.* London : Routledge, 1991.

Cross, G.W. and Jeffares, Norman, ed. *In Excited Reverie.* London : Macmillan, 1965.

Crystal, David. *The Cambridge Encyclopaedia of Language.* Cambridge : Cambridge University Press, 1987.

Daiches, Davis. *The Present Age.* London : The Crescent Press, 1958.

Donoghue, Denis. *The Third Voice.* New Jersey : Princeton University Press, 1966.

- - - Yeats. London : Fontana Modern Masters, 1971.

Drew, Elizabeth. *Discovering Drama.* London : Jonathan Cape, 1939.

Dukore, Bernard F. *Dramatic Theory and Criticism : Greeks to Grotowski.* New York : Holt, Rinchart and Winston, Inc. 1974.

Ellis Fermor, Una. *The Irish Dramatic Movement.* London : Methuen & Co. Ltd., 1954.

Elam, Keir. *Shakespeare's Universe of Discourse : Language Games in the Comedies.* Cambridge : Cambridge University Press, 1984.

Ellmann, Richard. *The Identity of Yeats.* London : Macmillan, 1954.

- - - *Yeats, The Man and the Masks.* London : Macmillan, 1949.

Enkvist, Nils Erik. *Linguistic Stylistics.* Paris : Mauton & Co., 1973.

Enkvist, Nils Erik, Spender John, Gregory Michael J. *Linguistics and Style.* London : Oxford University Press, 1964.

Esslin, Martin. *The Theatre of the absurd.* Penguin : Harmonds Worth, 1968.

Flannery, James. W. W.B. *Yeats and the Idia of a Theatre.* New Haven : Yale University Press, 1976.

Fowler, Roger, ed. *Style and Structure in Literature : Essays in the New Stylistics.* London : Basil Blackwell, 1975.

Ford, Boris, ed. *The Present.* vol. 8 of the *New Pelican Guide to English Literature.* Middlesex : Penguin Boods, 1983.

Fowler, Roger ed. *Essays on Style and Language.* London : Routledge and Kegan Paul, 1966.

Freeman, Donald C. ed. *Linguistics and Literary Style.* New York : Holt, Rinehart and Winston, Inc. 1970.

Fry, Northrop. *T.S. Eliot.* Edinburg and London : Oliver and Boyd, 1963.

Fraser, G.S. *The Modern Writer and His World.* England : Pelican Books, 1967.

Gallup, Donald. *T.S. Eliot* (A Biography). London : Faber and Faber Ltd., 1969.

Gardener, Helen. *The Art of T.S. Eliot.* London : The Crescent Press, M.C.M. 1969.

Gascoigne, Bamber. *Twentieth Century Drama.* London : Huchinson University Library, 1962.

Gassner, John. *Form and Idea in Modern Theatre.* New York and Dryden Press, 1956.

- - - *Masters of the Drama.* Third Revised adn enlarged edition. London : Dover Publication, Inc. 1954.

- - - *Theatre at the Cross-roads.* New York : Holt Rinehart and Winston, 1960.

Good, Maene. *W.B. Yeats and the Creation of the Tragic Universe.* London : Macmillan, 1986.

Gordon, G.S. ed. *English Literature and the Classics.* Oxford : Clarendon Press, 1912.

Gowda, Anniah H.H. *Dramatic Poetry (From Medieval to Modern Times).* Madrea : Macmillan, 1971.

- - - *The Revival of English Poetic Drama* Bangalore : The Government Press, 1963.

Gowda, H.H.A., Wells Henry W. *Style and Structure in Shakespeare*. New Delhi : Vikas Publishing House Pvt. Ltd., 1979.

Granville, Barker. *On Poetry in Drama : The Romanes Lecture*. London : Sidgwick and Jackson, 1937.

Greenwood, Ormesrod. *The Playwright*. London : Sir Isac Pitman and Sons Ltd., 1950.

Halliday, M.A.K., McIntosh Angus, Strevens Peter. *The Linguistic Sciences and Language Teaching*. London : Longman Group Ltd., 1964.

Hall, James and Martin, Steinmann, ed. *The Permanence of Yeats*. New York., 1964.

Hall, James and Martin, Steinmann, ed. *The Permanence of Yeats*. New York : Hill and Wang, 1960.

Harris Roy, Trans. *F de Saussure Course in General Linguistics*. London : Gerald Duckworth & Co. Ltd., 1983.

Henn, T.R. *The Lonely Tower*. London : Methuen, 1950.

Hinch Liffe, Arnold P. *T.S. Eliot : Plays : A Casebook*. London : Macmillan, 1985.

Hockett, Charles F. *A Course in Modern Linguistics*. New York : Macmillan, 1958.

Hone, Joseph. *W.B. Yeats (1865-1939)*. London : Macmillan, 1962.

Honigmann, E.A.J. *Shakespeare : Seven Tragedies*. London : Macmillan, 1976.

Hopper, Stanley, ed. *Spiritual Problems in Contemporary Literature* New York : Harper and Brothers, 1952.

Hough, Graham. *The Last Romantics*. London : Methuen and Co. Ltd., 1947.

- - - *Style and Stylistics*. London : Routledge and Kegan Paul, 1969.

Howarth, Herbert. *The Irish Writers*. New York : Hill and Wang, 1959.

- - - *Notes on Some Figures Behind T.S. Eliot*. Cambridge : The Riberside Press, 1964.

Hulme, Hilda M. *Explorations in Shakespeare's Language*. New York : Longman Inc., 1977.

Ishabashi, Hiro. "Yeats and the Noh", *Delmen Press Yeats Centenary Papers,* Number VI, MCMLXV, 1966.

James, Williams. *The Varieties of Religious Experience.* New York : The New American Library, 1961.

Jeffares Norman A. and Knowland A.S. *A Commentary on the Collected Plays of W.B. Yeats.* London : Macmillan, 1975.

Jeffares, Norman A. ed. *Yeats' Selected Plays.* London : Macmillan, 1964.

- - - W.B. Yeats : Man and Poet. London : Routledge and Kegan Paul, 1949.

Jones, D.E. *The Plays of T.S. Eliot.* London : Routledge and Kegan Paul, 1963.

Joos, Martin, ed. *Readings in Linguistics I.* London : The University of Chicago Press, 1957. 4th edn. 1966.

Katie. Wales. *Dictionary of Stylistics.* London : Longman, 1989.

Deene, Donald. *Twenty Plays of Noh Theatre.* New York and London : Columbia University Press, 1970.

Kenner, Hugh. *The Invisible Poet.* London : W.H. Allen, 1960.

Kitto, H.D.F. *Form and Meaning in Drama.* London : Methuesn, 1960.

- - - *T.S. Eliot.* Prentice Hall, Inc. Engelwood Cliff, N.J., 1962.

Knight, G. Wilson. *The Wheel of Fire.* London : Methuen, 1960.

Knights, L.C. *Explorations,* London. : Chatts and Windus, 1946.

Korg, Jacob. *Language in Modern Literature : Innovation and Experiment.* Sussex : The Harvester Press Ltd., 1979.

Krans, Horatio Sheafe. *William Butlere Yeats and the Irish Literary Revival.* New York : Haskell House, 1966.

Krishnaswami, N. *Introduction to Linguistics for Language Teachers.* Bombay : Somaiya Publications Pvt. Ltd., 1971.

Krishnaswami, N. and Verma, S.K. *Modern Linguistics : An Introduction.* Delhi : Oxford University Press, 1989.

Lucas, F.L. *The Decline and Fall of the Romantic Ideal.* Cambridge : Cambridge University Press, 1963.

- - - *Tragedy.* London : Hogarth Press, 1957.

Lumley, Frederick. *Trends in Twentieth Century Drama : A Survey since Ibsen and Shaw*. Rockliff, 1956.

Lyons, John. *New Horizons in Linguistics.* Middlesex : Penguin Books, 1970.

Malthiessen, F.O. *The Achievement of T.S. Eliot.* London : Routledge and Kegan Paul, 1960.

Miller, Liam, Ed. *The Dolmen Press Yeats Centenary Papers*. MCM LXV. The Dolmen Press Ltd., 1968.

Millward, Cetra. *Handbook for Writers.* New York : Holt. Ranehard and Winston, 1980.

Nathan, Lenonard E. *The Tragic Drama of William Butler Yeats.* New York : Columbia University Press, 1965.

Nevill Coghill, Intro. *The Family Reunion By T.S. Eliot.* Delhi : Oxford University Press, 1963.

- - - Intro, *Murder int he Cathedral by T.S. Eliot.* Delhi : Oxford University Press, 1963.

Nicoll, Allardyce. *British Drama.* London, George G. Harrap & Co. Ltd., 1925.

- - - *The Theory of Drama.* London : George G. Harrap & Co. Ltd. 1969.

- - - *A History of English Drama.* 3 vols. Cambridge : Cambridge University Press, 1946.

Parkin, Andrew. *The Dramatic Imagination of W.B. Yeats.* Dublin : Gill and Macmillan etc., 1978.

Partridge, A.C. *The Language of Renaissance Poetry.* London : Andre Deutisch Limited, 1971.

Pathak, R.S. ed. *New Directions in Eliot Studies.* New Delhi : Northern Book Centre, 1990.

Peacock, Ronald. *The Poet in the Theatre.* London : Routledge and Kegan Paul, 1946.

Pei. Mario. *Glossary of Linguistic Terminology.* New York : Columbia University Press, 1966.

Perrin, Lawrence. *Sound and Sense : An Introduction to Poetry.* New York : Hartcourt, Brace and World, 1956.

Petyt, K.M. *The Study of Dialect : An Introduction to Dialectology.* London : Andre Deutsch Ltd., 1980.

Pinchliffe, Arnold P. ed. *Drama Criticism : Developments Since Ibsen.* A Casehood. London : Macmillan, 1979.

Preminger, Alex, ed. *Encyclopaedia of Poetry and Poetics*. Princeton : Princeton University Press, 1965.

Prickett, Stephen, ed. *The Romantics.* London : Mathuen, 1981.

Rajan, Balchandran. *W.B. Yeats : A Critical Introduction.* London : Hutchinson University Library Press, 1965.

Robbins. Rossell Hope. *The T.S. Eliot Myth.* New York : Henry Schuman, 1951.

Robson, W.W. *Modern English Literature.* Middlesex : Oxford University Press, 1970.

Ronsley, Joseph, ed. *Yeats' Autobiography : Life ad Symbolic Pattern.* Middlesex : Oxford University Press, 1968.

Sapir, Edward. *Languages : An Introduction to the Study of Speech.* London : Harcourt, Brace & World Inc., 1949.

Sarkar, Subhas. *T.S. Eliot, the Dramatist.* Calcutta : The Minerva Associates, 1973.

Sebeok, Thomas A., ed. *Style and Language.* Cambridge : MIT Press, 1960.

Skene, Reg. *The Cuchulain Plays of W.B. Yeats : A Study.* London : Macmillan, 1974.

Smith, Carol H. *T.S. Eliot's Dramatic Theory and Practice.* Princeton : Princeton University Press, 1967.

Smith, Grover. *T.S. Eliot's Poetry and Plays.* Chicago : The University of Chicago Press, 1960.

Speaight, Robert. *Drama since 1939.* London : Longmans, Green & Co, 1947.

Spender, Stephen. *Eliot.* Glassgow : Frontana/Collins, 1975.

Soitzer, Leo. *Linguistics and Literary History.* Princeton : Princeton University Press, 1948.

Stapleton, Michael. *The Cambridge Guide to English Literature.* Cambridge : Cambridge University Press, 1983.

Stead, C.K. *Pound, Yeats, Eliot and the Modernist Movement.* London : Macmillan, 1985.

Taylor, Richard. *A Reader's Guide to the Plays of W.B. Yeats.* London : Macmillan, 1984.

--- *The Drama of W.B. Yeats : Irish Myth and the Japanese Noh.* London : Yale University Press, 1976.

Thoulers, Priscilla. *Modern Poetic Drama.* Oxford : Basil Blackwell, 1934.

Ytrein, J.C. *Drama (1945-1950).* London : Longmans Green and Co., 1951.

Trudgill, Peter. *Socio Linguistics.* Middlesex : Penguin Books Ltd., 1974.

Turner, G.W. *Stylistics.* Middlesex : Penguin, 1973.

Unger, Leonard. ed. *T.S. Eliot : A Selected Critique.* New York : Rinehard & Co., Inc. 1948.

Unterecker, John. *A Reader's Guide to William Bulter Yeats.* London : Thames and Hudson, 1959.

--- *Yeats : A Collection of Critical Essays.* London : Prentice Hall, 1982.

Ure, Peter. Towards A Mythology. New York : State of New York Press, 1946.

--- *Yeats, the Playwright.* London : Oliver and Boys, 1963.

--- *Yeats and Anglo-Irish Literature : Critical Essays.* Liverpool : Liverpool University Press, 1974.

Vendler, H.H. *Yeats' Vision and the Later Plays.* Cambridge, Mass : Harvard University Press, 1963.

Wade, Allen, ed. *The Letters of W.B. Yeats.* London : Rupert Hart Davis, 1954.

Wallwork, J.F. *Language and Linguistics : An Introduction to the Study of Language.* London : Heinemann Educational Books 1969.

Ward, A.C. *Longman Companion to Twentieth Century Literature, 1970.* Essex : Longman Group Ltd., 3rd edn., 1981.

Word, David. *T.S. Eliot between two Worlds : A Reading of T.S. Eliot's Poetry and Plays.* London : Routledge and Kegan Paul, 1973.

Warren, Austin and Wellek, Rene. *Theory of Literature.* London : Jonathan Cape, 1949.

Wartburg, Walter V. *Problems and Methods in Linguistics.* London : Oxford Basil Blackwell, 1969.

Wells, Henry W. *The Classic Drama of the Orient.* Bombay : Asia Publishing House, 1965.

Williamson, Goerge. *A Reader's Guide to T.S. Eliot.* London : Thames and Hudson, 1955.

Wilsion, F.A.C. *Yeats' Iconography.* London : Gollancz, 1960.

--- W.B. *Yeats and Tradition.* London : Gollance, 1958.

Worth, Catharine. *The Irish Drama of Europe from Yeats to Beckett.* London : The Alhlone Press, 1986.

Wrenn, C.L. "T.S. Eliot and the Language of Poetry", *Word and Symbol : Studies in English Language.* London : Longman, Green & Co. Ltd., 1967.

Yule, George. *The Study of Language.* Cambridge : Cambridge University Press, 1985.

ARTICLES IN PERIODICALS

Daveport, Gasy D. "Eliot's the Cocktail Party : Comic Perspective and Salvation," *Modern Drama,* XVII, 3 (Sept. 1974).

Gautam, Kripa K. "The Linguistic Identity of The Absured in Pinter's The Birth day Party", *Rajasthan University Studies in English,* XIX (1987), 91-100.

Gorsky, Susan R. "A Ritual Drama : Yeats' Plays for Dancers," *Modern Drama* XVII, 2 (July 1974).

Hawkins, A. Desmond. "The Poet in the Theatre." *The Criterion,* XIV, LIV (Oct. 1934).

Helming, Steven. "The Success and Failure of T.S. Eliot", *The Sewanee Review,* XCVI, I (Jan-March, 1988).

Heyningen, Christina Van. "The Plays of H.W.D. Manson", *The Journal of Commonwealth Literature.* VI, 1, (June 1971). Oxford University Press for the University of Leads.

Johnson, Martha. "Reflections of Inner Life : Masks and Masked Acting in Ancient Greek Tragedy and Japanese Noh Drama," *Modern Drama,* XXXV, I (March 1992).

Kim, Myung Whan. "Dance and Rhythm : Their Meaning in Yeats and Noh." *Modern Drama,* XV, I (May 1972).

Kirkley, Richard. Bruce. "A Catch in the Breath : Language and Consciousness in Samuel Beckett's... but the Clouds..." *Modern Drama,* XXXV, 2 (Dec. 1992).

Koritz, Amy. "Women Dancing : The Structure of Gender in Yeats' Early Plays for Dancers," *Modern Drama,* XXXII, 3 (Sept. 1989).

Newton, Norman, "Yeats as Dramatist : The Player Queen," *Essays in Criticism,* 8 : 269-284 (July 1958).

Prior, Moody E. "Yeats' Search for a Dramatic From", *Tri-Quarterly,* 4 (1965) 112-14.

Patrides, C.A. "T.S. Eliot : Alliance of Levity and Serious-ness," *The Sewance Review*, XCVI, I (Jan-march 1988)

Rajan, Balchandran. "Yeats and the Absured," *Tri-Quarterly,* 4 (1965) 130-37.

Suheil, Bushrei. "Yeats : The Poet as Hero," *Essays and Studies,* The English Association, 1982.

Spurr, David. "T.S. Eliot's Divided Criticals Sensibilities," *Criticism : A Quarterly for Literature and Art*, XXIII, I (Winter 1981).

Tate, Allen, ed. *The Sewanee Review* (A Special Issue on T.S. Eliot), LXXIV, 11 (Jan-March 1966).

Ure, Peter, "Yeats' Cristian Mystery Plays," *Review of English Studies,* New Series, 11 : 171-182 (May 1960).